Mt. McKinley
Climber's Handbook

Mt. McKinley Climber's Handbook

By Glenn Randall

with photographs by

Bradford Washburn

Chockstone Press
Evergreen, Colorado

ISBN: 0-934641-55-2

COVER PHOTOS BY GLENN RANDALL: (front) Denali from the toe, Souheast Ridge of Mt. Foraker. (back top) Bob Stanton and Mt McKinley from the west fork of the Kahiltna Glacier. (back bottom) Bill Miller at 17,000 feet on the West Buttress Route.

All uncredited photos by Glenn Randall.

PUBLISHED AND DISTRIBUTED BY:
CHOCKSTONE PRESS, INC.
Post Office Box 3505
Evergreen, Colorado 80439

Acknowledgements

The second edition of this book has benefited greatly from the thoughtful criticism provided by several experts on North America's greatest mountain. Dr. Peter Hackett, one of the nation's foremost authorities on altitude illness, read the medical chapter. The Denali National Park mountaineering rangers, particularly Jim Phillips and Scott Gill, plowed through entire manuscript and helped me update many sections. For their patience and care, I owe them my thanks. I would also like to thank Harry Johnson again. Harry was instrumental in bringing the first edition of this book to press. And finally, I must thank Cora Randall, my wife, for her insightful critique of the manuscript. Her comments improved its clarity and readability immensely.

Table Of Contents

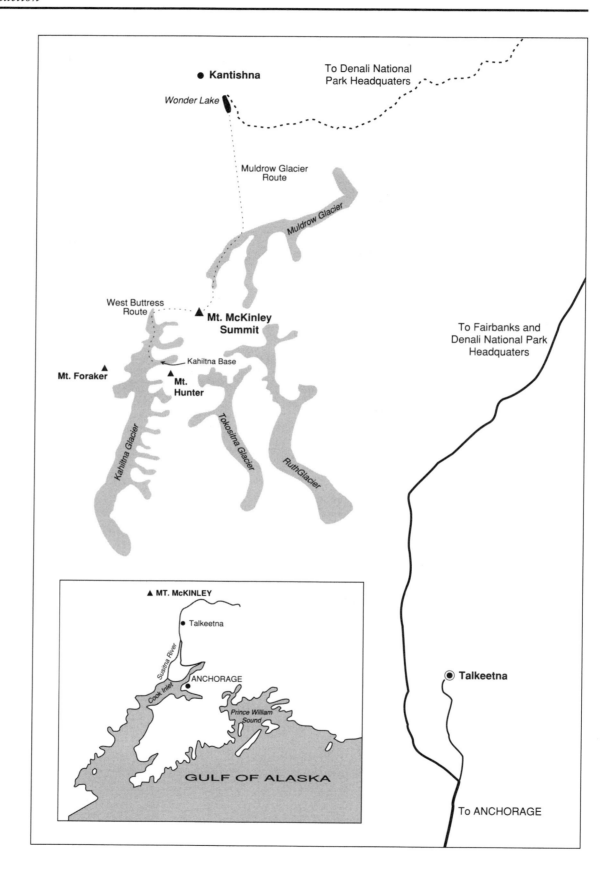

Introduction

BY EVERY MEASURE BUT EXTREME ALTITUDE, Mt. McKinley is one of the world's greatest mountains. Only a collision of continental plates could have created its stupendous bulk. McKinley began to rise some 65 million years ago when the Pacific Plate, the enormous, drifting chunk of the earth's crust that underlies the Pacific Ocean, collided with the also-drifting American Plate. Two nearly unstoppable forces had met head-on, and something had to give. The edge of the Pacific Plate dove toward the earth's center, and the American Plate buckled up, heaving the granite of the Alaska Range 20,320 feet into the sky.

From the north, McKinley's walls leap 18,000 feet above Wonder Lake in a horizontal distance of only 27 miles. From the snout of the Peters Glacier, at 3,000 feet, to the summit is only 12 miles. Perhaps no other mountain in the world rises so far in such a short horizontal distance. McKinley's southern flank rises 13,200 feet above the glacier landing site from which the most popular routes start. From Mount Everest's base camp to its summit is 2,000 feet less.

Subarctic Mt. McKinley, 63 degrees north of the equator, rises out of a sprawling web of glaciers whose tongues push into the lowlands to an elevation of 1,000 feet. In the Himalayas, at the latitude of Miami, the glacier systems extend down only to 13,500 feet. The climate only halfway to McKinley's summit is as severe as the North Pole's. Nighttime temperatures two-thirds of the way up McKinley frequently hit 30 degrees below zero Fahrenheit during May, the peak climbing season. Not until Himalayan climbers are nearly twice that high do they experience such extremes. The northern latitude means the oxygen content in the air on McKinley's summit is equivalent to the oxygen available on the summit of a Himalayan peak that is 800 to 1,500 feet higher, according to data published by the National Oceanic and Atmospheric Administration. Just six months after climbing Mount Everest, Himalayan veteran Doug Scott wrote that McKinley was equivalent to a 24,000-foot Himalayan peak.

These declarations can only suggest the power, majesty and stunning beauty that have drawn mountaineers to McKinley from all over the world for nearly 100 years. McKinley is the ultimate challenge in North American mountaineering. Already it has claimed 75 lives. Like many climbers, I have learned the hard way that the Alaska Range is terribly unforgiving of inexperience, ignorance and poor judgment. It is my hope that this handbook will help mountaineers enjoy a safe climb on this magnificent peak.

*A member of the 1913
Hudson Stuck expedition
climbs toward the south
summit of McKinley.*
Photo: Hudson Stuck

Men and Mt. McKinley

LONG BEFORE WHITE MEN had ever heard of Alaska, the natives of the interior had a name for the majestic ice mountain that dominated the southern skyline. They called it Denali, "The High One." Denali it remained until prospector William Dickey traveled in its shadow in 1896. He named it McKinley after William McKinley, the Republican nominee for president in 1896, and returned to civilization convinced that it was the highest mountain in North America. The name stuck, at least as far as the U.S. Geological Survey was concerned. Many mountaineers, Alaskans and the Alaskan Board of Geographic Names, however, use Denali.

Dickey's article in a New York newspaper sparked an interest in exploring, measuring and even climbing this subarctic giant. Dr. Frederick Cook circumnavigated the peak in 1903; in 1906, Cook disappeared into the wilderness for 12 days with one companion. He returned claiming the first ascent. His companion refused to corroborate his claim, however, and doubt began to grow. Cook's claim was disproved once and for all when skeptics showed that his "summit photos" were actually taken atop an insignificant bump along the Ruth Glacier.

In 1910, while the Cook controversy was still sizzling, four Alaskan sourdoughs, veterans of many an Alaskan winter, decided to disprove Cook by climbing the mountain themselves. By March 25, they had driven a dog team to 11,000 feet, and arrived at the head of the Muldrow Glacier. After exploring for a way around the gigantic icefall at the Muldrow's head, later named the Harper Icefall, William Taylor, Pete Anderson and Charles McGonagall decided to launch a one-day summit bid while Tom Lloyd remained in camp. Encumbered with a 14-foot spruce pole, which they naively hoped would be visible from Fairbanks when they planted it on the summit, they left camp at 11,000 feet at 3 a.m. on April 10. They each carried a pack containing a thermos of hot chocolate and half a dozen doughnuts. Disdaining a rope, with crude crampons they called creepers lashed to their oversized moccasins, they climbed more than 8,000 feet in a single day. At 19,000 feet, they planted the spruce pole. McGonagall turned back, but Taylor and Anderson struggled up the final rise of Pioneer Ridge to the 19,470-foot summit of the north peak. They descended all the way to their high camp without accident, a remarkable bit of luck considering the crevasses in the Harper Glacier. Billy Taylor still had three doughnuts left.

Unfortunately for the sourdoughs, they had chosen to ascend the lower of McKinley's two summits. The south summit rises 850 feet higher. Had they known which summit was higher, they would probably have pulled off one of the most astonishing first ascents in mountaineering history. As it was, no one would come close to matching their one-day summit sprint until 1978, when Ned Gillette and Galen Rowell reached the true summit in one day from Kahiltna Pass, on the west side of the mountain at 10,000 feet. Rowell and Gillette, exhausted, did not complete their descent in one day. Instead, they took advantage of the shelter kindly offered by friends encamped at 17,200 feet, then completed their descent in haste the next day as Rowell began developing pulmonary edema. In 1986, Australian climber Gary Scott climbed from the Kahiltna Base landing strip at 7,200 feet to the summit via the West Buttress in 18½ hours. The key to his success, aside from incredible fitness, was the acclimatization he developed by spending a month at 14,300 feet as the volunteer manager of the rescue camp.

The Episcopal Archdeacon of the Yukon, Hudson Stuck, led the first ascent of the south summit in 1913, three years after the Sourdough expedition. Stuck, who was almost 50 at the time, chose Harry P. Karstens, Robert G. Tatum and Walter Harper as his companions. Stuck was determined to leave nothing to chance. Many of their supplies were carried in by water the previous summer and cached 50 miles from the mountain. They made their own ice axes and crampons. For boots, they wore moccasins with five pairs of socks. For bedding, they had down quilts, camel's hair blankets and a 25-pound wolf robe. Starting in the middle of March with dog teams, they relayed a ton and a half of food and gear 50 miles to the base of the mountain's north side.

The Sourdoughs' 1910 one-day summit assault was not matched until 1978. Standing from left to right: Charles McGonagall, Pete Anderson, William Taylor. Seated: Tom Lloyd.

At their camp on Cache Creek they paused to hunt caribou and make pemmican, cooked, minced meat rolled into a ball with melted butter, salt and pepper. The sun-dried hides of the caribou became their sleeping pads.

Like the Sourdoughs, they drove a dog team all the way to the head of the Muldrow, even carting in firewood. Above the Muldrow's head, however, caution and the debris of a massive earthquake in 1912 forced them to adopt the expeditionary tactics that remain traditional on McKinley to this day. The earthquake had rendered Karstens Ridge, the easiest path to the mountain's upper reaches, vastly more broken and difficult than when the Sourdoughs scampered up it three years before. The team hewed a three-mile long staircase in the snow and ice, then began relaying loads to the Harper Glacier at about 14,500 feet.

On June 7, almost two months after beginning their expedition, they left their high camp at 17,500 feet, climbed to Denali Pass and struggled on to the summit. Stuck wrote later, "Only those who have for long years cherished a great and almost inordinate desire, and have had that desire gratified to the limit of their expectation, can enter into the deep thankfulness and content that filled the heart upon the descent of this mountain." Nineteen years passed before men stood once again on McKinley's summit.

In 1952, Bradford Washburn, director of the Boston Museum of Science, made the first ascent of the West Buttress. It was the first time the mountain had been climbed by a route other than the Muldrow. Already, Washburn was deep into aerial photography and mapping, which not only revealed the possibility of climbing the mountain from its west side, but also a score of other routes that would be climbed, one by one, in the years that followed.

Two years later, a bold team of four led by National Park Service Ranger Elton Thayer climbed McKinley's South Buttress. They started from the Alaska Railroad at Curry, received an airdrop at the head of the Ruth Glacier and relayed loads up the South Buttress, around the southwest face of the summit pyramid through Thayer Basin and up the ridge dividing Thayer Basin and the Harper Glacier. The day after reaching the summit they descended the Harper Glacier and started down Karstens Ridge. Thayer slipped on the ice, and the others could not arrest his fall. Roped together, they tumbled 800 feet or more. Thayer was killed, and George Argus broke his hip. Morton Wood and Les Viereck managed to lower Argus 1,000 feet down to the head of the Muldrow and hike out to Wonder Lake for help. A rescue helicopter eventually carried Argus to the hospital that would be his home for several months.

Five years later, in 1959, a team of four climbed the West Rib, which rises out of the northeast fork of the Kahiltna Glacier at 10,500 feet and intersects the summit plateau at 19,500 feet, just below Kahiltna Horn. These climbers made full use of their limited supply of fixed rope by fixing the climb in sections. On the descent, they left the West Rib at about 16,000 feet and traversed to the West Buttress, continuing down to Kahiltna Base by that route.

Washburn's aerial reconnaissance had produced a number of photos of the most direct line to McKinley's summit, a spur in the center of the south face soon to be known as the Cassin Ridge. In 1961, a six-man Italian team led by famous alpinist Riccardo Cassin chose a direct line up the crest of the ridge, tackling several difficult rock sections that later parties would avoid. After three weeks of pushing the route ahead, fixing ropes and bringing up supplies, all six climbers stuffed themselves into two tiny tents at their high camp at 17,000 feet. Early on July 19 they launched their summit bid. Seventeen hours later, in a driving wind, they finally reached the summit. Not until 6 a.m. the next morning did they regain their high camp. Jack Canali, who was wearing single boots of leather, had severe frostbite. His feet swelled so much while the team rested at the high camp that he could not put his boots on again. Another team member, Gigi Alippi, loaned Canali his boots, then swaddled his own feet in four pairs of socks and boot covers. Unable to wear crampons, Alippi slipped during the descent and dragged his rope mate off the route. Miraculously, Cassin caught them both. At last, after 75 hours of continuous snowfall, the weather cleared. Five days after reaching the summit, the entire team reached their base camp on the northeast fork of the Kahiltna. The team dragged Canali to the landing site on an improvised sled, where a glacier pilot evacuated him.

In 1967, a team of eight climbers set out to make the first winter ascent of McKinley. No one knew what extremes of temperature and wind would be found on McKinley's summit in February. The climbers did know they would have only nine and a half hours of daylight, compared to the essentially unbroken daylight available in June. On January 31, the third day of the climb up the West Buttress, Jacques Batkin, a powerful and very experienced French climber, fell unroped into a crevasse on the lower Kahiltna Glacier and died. By mutual agreement, the team had been ferrying loads unroped. They had discovered at great cost that not even a hard-packed glacier surface eliminates the danger of hidden crevasses.

After several days of agonizing debate, they decided to go on. On February 28, at 7 p.m., Art Davidson, Ray Genet and Dave Johnston stood on the summit. The temperature was –58 degrees F; the wind, 20 knots. In total blackness, they began the descent.

At midnight, they reached Denali Pass, 18,200 feet. Exhausted and with steep ice below, they decided to bivouac rather than descend the final 1,000 feet to their friends in the snow cave at their high camp.

By dawn, the wind was blowing 130 miles per hour. Frantically, they dug a cave, losing packs and foam pads in the process. For three days the wind continued unabated. They ate their final bite of food and used up their last ounce of gasoline. Frostbite set in as their bodies dehydrated and ran out of fuel to combat the –40 degree F cold. On the fourth day, Genet volunteered to try to find the gallon of gas that Johnston had cached some 200 feet away almost three years before. Johnston had spotted it on an unsuccessful attempt at the summit a few days before they reached the top.

Unable to stand in the ferocious winds, Genet crawled to the spot Johnston had described and found the can still there. His hazardous journey had probably saved their lives.

The wind abated at last. After six days in the cave, scarcely able to stand, the three wasted mountaineers crawled outside and started down, their frozen feet screaming in pain with every step. Their companions had abandoned the 17,200-foot camp, knowing the summit team's chances of survival were slim. Unwilling to relinquish all hope, however, the teammates had left a small supply of food, which renewed the summit team's strength. They descended further. The camp at 14,300 feet was also empty. Finally, at Windy Corner, a search plane spotted them. A few hours later, they were aboard a helicopter en route to an Anchorage hospital.

Johnston was hospitalized for 45 days, bedridden for another 16. He eventually lost parts of three toes. Davidson lost one toe and partial use of three others. Genet's feet, on the other hand, healed in about three weeks.

Four months after the winter climb, a three-pronged expedition organized by Boyd Everett climbed not only the Cassin Ridge and the South Buttress, but also pioneered a new route up the steepest part of the south face between the two. Much of the first ascent of the American Direct took place during a 13-day storm, during which the four-man team was hit by avalanches "on the run, while asleep and with their pants down," as Roman Laba wrote later in the American Alpine Journal. None of the avalanches swept anyone away, and the entire team reached the summit at midnight, August 4.

1967 was also the year when McKinley claimed seven lives in a single storm. On July 17, the single worst disaster in McKinley's history began when six inexperienced members of the Wilcox Expedition got a late start for the summit and bivouacked at about 19,500 feet rather than retreat. The next day only five felt like continuing. The sixth awaited their return at the bivouac. The five reached the summit safely, but were caught by a severe windstorm on the descent. All six died. A seventh climber, waiting in the high camp below, also was killed when his tent on the Harper Glacier was destroyed by high winds.

The number of climbers who attempted McKinley each year increased steadily during the '60s. In 1970, the boom really began. By 1971, there was so much garbage on the West Buttress that a seven-member team received a grant from the American Alpine Club to clean up the route. The team carried down 200 pounds of paper and 180 pounds of cans and foil. They by no means got it all.

In the early days, dogs were used on McKinley expeditions.
Photo: Merl La Voy

The '70s and '80s saw many real accomplishments, although a few of the feats bordered on the hare-brained. In 1970, world-famous Japanese adventurer Naomi Uemura made the first solo of the West Buttress. Two years later the West Rib received its first alpine-style ascent, in which the route was climbed without fixed ropes and without relaying loads. In 1976, four hang-glider pilots dragged their 20-foot long, 60-pound gliders to the summit and took off. Three made it. One didn't. He crashed on takeoff and tumbled 800 feet down the south face. In 1979, Charlie Porter soloed the Cassin. That same year, Genet helped Joe Reddington, father of the 1,000-mile Iditarod Dog Sled Race from Anchorage to Nome, take a team of huskies to the summit of McKinley. The Cassin received its first winter ascent in 1982. This was only the second time the mountain had been climbed in winter by any route. In 1984, Uemura returned and made the first winter solo ascent of the mountain via the West Buttress. His diet consisted of raw caribou, seal oil and dried fruit. He died, probably of hypothermia, exhaustion and perhaps a fall, during the descent from the summit to his 17,200-foot high camp.

Throughout the 1980s, various teams picked off new lines and variations on all sides of the mountain. In 1984, Italian mountaineer Renato Casarotto tackled

McKinley's last major untouched spur, the Ridge of No Return, on the south side of the South Buttress. As always, he climbed alone, belaying himself with a 300-foot rope. The system required him to lead each section without his pack, rappel or climb down the section, then climb it again carrying his load. His wife waited in a snowcave on the Ruth Glacier. Casarotto took two falls on the wickedly corniced half-mile-long knife-edge that was the crux of the route and was astonished when his self-belay system held him. After 12 days, he reached the crest of the South Buttress at 15,000 feet, then descended the South Buttress to the East Fork of the Kahiltna and on to Kahiltna Base, narrowly escaping death in a hidden crevasse when he broke through to his waist. Upon arriving at base camp, he cleaned out the radio operator's food supply and fell asleep in a lawn chair in the sun.

In 1991, Mugs Stump, a highly experienced guide, traversed from the West Buttress at 14,300 feet to the West Rib, descended the West Rib to the Northeast Fork of the Kahiltna Glacier and soloed the Cassin Ridge in the astounding time of 15 hours from the base of the Japanese Couloir to the summit ridge. He descended the West Buttress, reaching his camp at 14,300 feet again 27 hours and 30 minutes after he left, completing perhaps the most impressive "one-day" feat ever recorded on McKinley. Such solo heroics make inspiring stories, but they can easily lure the unwary into thinking that the mountain is less formidable than it is. One year later, Stump was killed in a crevasse fall while guiding an expedition on the South Buttress. His death was one of 11 fatalities on McKinley that season, making 1992 the most tragic year ever in the mountain's long, savage history.

Are You Ready For McKinley?

I F THIS WAS A HIKING GUIDEBOOK or even a guide to Colorado's fourteeners, it would probably seem presumptuous to title a chapter, "Are You Ready for This?" So many climbers, however, have underestimated McKinley at great cost to themselves, rescuers and American taxpayers that I think the question needs to be raised.

How much experience should a climber have before attempting McKinley? It's unrealistic to give an answer like, "Ten ascents of 14,000-foot peaks." Summer strolls up fourteeners in Colorado or California do little to provide the skills McKinley climbers need. Learning to climb high-angled rock and waterfall ice is necessary preparation only for the difficult technical routes. Most falls on McKinley occur during the descent, when someone trips over his crampons on a 30- to 50-degree snow slope and fails to self-arrest, not when someone blows a 5.10 move or peels off a sheet of vertical water ice. Ten winter ascents of major Colorado peaks or northeastern peaks like Mt. Washington, site of the world's highest recorded wind speed (231 mph), would be much better preparation, particularly if the climbs are deliberately extended over several days to gain experience in the art of remaining comfortable while camping in severe cold and wind. Extensive practice cramponing up and, particularly, down, steep hard summer snowfields while carrying a substantial pack may be the closest that mountaineers in the Lower 48 can come to simulating the type of climbing most commonly found on McKinley. Spending time on the glaciated mountains of the Northwest practicing glacier travel and crevasse rescue skills would also be valuable.

Previous high-altitude experience (above 15,000 feet) is desirable but not essential. However, climbers who have never gone beyond the 14,495-foot height of California's Mt. Whitney, highest mountain in the Lower 48, should definitely be cautious about hurrying up McKinley, where they will normally have to camp at over 17,000 feet, usually for several days. Most climbers feel fine when they climb to the summit of a 14,000-foot peak in the Lower 48 and spend half an hour there enjoying the view before descending rapidly. They conclude that they will also feel fine hurrying up to 14,000 feet on McKinley and camping there for several days. As hundreds of altitude-sick climbers can testify, however, that's rarely the case. McKinley is an order of magnitude more demanding than any peak in the Lower 48.

Training for McKinley should be undertaken as seriously as the climb itself. The atmospheric pressure at Denali Pass, 18,200 feet, is only half that of sea-level. Each quart of air you gulp at Denali Pass contains only half the oxygen of a quart you inhale while soaking up rays on the beach. From the West Buttress high camp to the summit is an elevation gain of over 3,000 feet. For most people, the summit day starts at an altitude where simply pulling on their boots makes them pant.

The Sourdoughs set an impressive example of fitness during their first ascent of the North Peak that has only rarely been equaled since. The crippling accident that cut down two unfit and unwise climbers in 1976 shows what can happen to those whose bodies are ill-prepared but who push on regardless.

At 4:30 a.m. on May 10, four climbers left the West Buttress high camp at 17,200 feet. After six hours, twice as long as is usual, they finally reached Denali Pass, only 1,000 feet above their camp. Despite their sluggish pace, they continued. By 5:00 p.m. they had reached only 19,500 feet. At this point, two climbers wisely chose to descend and regained their camp safely. The other two, however, continued to the summit and bivouacked only 200 feet below it. They lost their bivouac sacks and did not use their stove. By morning, one of the pair was frostbitten and both were exhausted. During the descent they took a bad fall, then bivouacked again at 19,500 feet. They survived only because the weather was fair, and because two climbers descending the West Buttress after an ascent of the south face notified the remainder of their group that the summit pair was in extremely serious trouble. Fortunately, the summit pair's companions were able to reach them and help them down.

Aerobic fitness, most important on McKinley, is defined as the ability to take in, transport and utilize oxygen. One of the best measures of aerobic fitness, then, is the maximum amount of oxygen you can take in and use per minute. Since heavier people use more oxygen, maximum oxygen uptake is usually expressed in milliliters of oxygen consumed per kilogram of body weight per minute, or ml/kg/min. To estimate your maximum oxygen uptake, run as far as possible in 15 minutes. Record the distance run in meters (1 mile equals 1609 meters). Running on a track of known circumference makes estimating the distance easy. Divide the distance in meters by 15 to find speed in meters per minute. Your maximum oxygen uptake is approximately:

$$\text{MaxVO2} = ((\text{speed in meters per minute minus } 133) \times .172) + 33.3$$

Minimally fit people score around 40. Champion endurance athletes score in the 70s and 80s.

Ideally, you should train in a way that will approximate as closely as possible the effort you will demand of yourself on the mountain. Hiking in the hills with a heavy pack for eight to ten hours a day is probably the best training for McKinley. Unfortunately, few people can commit that much time except on weekends. Conversely, training by running the 100-yard dash will help you only to get out of your tent if you accidentally set it on fire. Sports that guarantee a high, sustained heart rate are the best preparation for McKinley. Hiking, cycling, cross-country skiing and running, particularly over hilly terrain, are all excellent because they train not only the heart and lungs, but also those muscles that will be taxed most heavily on the mountain. Swimming, while great for the heart and lungs, should be supplemented by training that works the legs in ways similar to mountaineering. Intermittently strenuous sports like tennis and racquetball are good only if played hard enough that the heart rate goes up and stays up for the entire game.

Everyone has a "training threshold," the minimum intensity and duration of training that stimulates their body to adapt. The more slack your body, the lower your training threshold. The more taut your body, the higher the threshold. To keep making progress, increases in the intensity and duration of your training are essential. Brian J. Sharkey, author of *Physiology of Fitness* (Human Kinetics Books, 1990), gives this rule of thumb for estimating your training zone, the range of heart rates that will produce a training effect. The lower limit is:

Heart rate = 55% (max heart rate – resting heart rate) + resting heart rate

The upper limit is:

Heart rate = 70% (max heart rate – resting heart rate) + resting heart rate

Your maximum heart rate is about 220 minus your age. To determine your exercise heart rate, take your pulse for 10 seconds immediately after you stop exercising. Sense your pulse with your fingertips at either your wrist or the carotid artery in your neck (just below the hinge of your jaw). Then multiply by six to get beats per minute. For a 25-year-old with a resting heart rate of 70, the training zone ranges approximately from 140 to 160 beats per minute.

If you are in poor condition now, a workout lasting only 15 minutes may be enough to nudge your body over the training threshold. As you get more fit, extend the workouts until you can train comfortably for 45 minutes to an hour or more.

Working out every other day is the minimum for gaining the fitness required for McKinley. Six days a week is preferable. Alternating hard workouts with easier ones helps avoid injury and gives your body time to recover and strengthen after each workout. Using an intense burst of effort for about one-twentieth of the workout (for example, by picking up the pace for the last quarter-mile of a five-mile run), gives the heart and lungs a useful added training stimulus. To keep track of your progress, record your workouts in a training log.

Aerobic fitness is the most important kind of fitness for McKinley, but upper-body strength should not be ignored. Simply picking up a heavy pack a dozen times a day demands a fair degree of power. More importantly, upper body strength provides the reserve of power required to get out of a crevasse with ascenders. Upper-body workouts two or three times a week in a weight room are probably the fastest way to develop the necessary strength. The workout should stress all muscles in the torso to encourage balanced, even development.

People who are minimally fit may be able to coax the necessary changes out of their bodies in three to six months if they train hard and manage to avoid injury. The ability to work hard for long periods continues to improve even after six months of steady training. Continued training is essential to maintain a high level of fitness once it is achieved.

Bill Miller carries a load at 16,600 feet on the West Buttress.
Photo: Glenn Randall

The best chance of success on the mountain will always belong to those best prepared physically. Though determination and a willingness to suffer have gotten many people to the top who could not have gotten there on fitness alone, people who try to climb the mountain on minimal fitness and maximum guts are operating within a very thin safety margin. If all of their companions are in similar shape, disaster may develop out of one simple mistake.

As you focus on preparing your body for McKinley, don't neglect any small, nagging medical problems you may have. The stress of a McKinley expedition can easily aggravate old knee and back injuries. In particular, consider seeing a dentist before embarking on your trip. Something that's easily cured in the city, such as a bad toothache, could force you to descend.

Again and again, people have underestimated the demands that McKinley will place on them. Fitness is one of the most important factors in meeting those demands. Fitness doesn't necessarily mean, however, that you can or should climb the mountain faster. Being in shape does not provide protection from acute mountain sickness. Instead, fitness makes a trip more enjoyable, safer and more likely to succeed. Those reasons alone are more than sufficient to start a training program, then stick with it.

The bottom line, in mountaineering as in other potentially dangerous sports, is good judgment. No matter what their abilities, climbers with good judgment who discover their skills are insufficient will retreat before they find themselves teetering on the brink of disaster. Climbers with bad judgment, no matter how skilled or experienced, can and have climbed themselves into trouble by pushing beyond even their well-developed capabilities.

It's as important to find well-prepared, compatible climbing partners as it is to prepare yourself. Team size, inevitably, is a compromise. Teams of two are fastest on technical terrain, but are extremely vulnerable to any accident or illness, particularly on remote routes and during glacier approaches. It's almost impossible for one climber to carry another to safety. It can be almost impossible for a climber working alone to pull his injured partner out of a crevasse. Leaving a sick or injured climber to go get help is a terrifying proposition for both the climber left behind and his partner, who usually must negotiate technical terrain and crevassed glaciers by himself. Teams of three or more provide a much greater margin of safety, although they move more slowly.

Every year, a handful of climbers attempt to solo McKinley. For good reason, the National Park Service strongly discourages this practice. Crevasses on Alaskan glaciers are frequently so well disguised that even the most experienced climbers fail to recognize them. Crevasse falls are common even on the popular routes. A crevasse fall that is only a minor annoyance to a roped team could easily be fatal to a soloist. Wise soloists make arrangements to travel with another party for the approach over the lower glaciers. Even after taking this elementary precaution, soloists still face much higher risks than teams of two or more. Soloing is not recommended.

Climbers should also consider carefully the problem of compatibility. Close quarters, high altitude, exhaustion, the need to make every decision together and the difficulty (and foolishness) of getting very far in front of or behind your partners all combine to stress even the closest friendships. Glacier pilot Jim Okonek once told me a story about flying in to the Ruth Glacier to pick up two climbers after they had finished their route. He found them sitting on the glacier half a mile apart. After taxiing up to the first climber, he asked, "Ready to go?" The climber nodded assent. "What about him?" Okonek asked, gesturing towards the climber's partner. "I don't know," said the climber. "You'll have to talk to him." With apparent reluctance, the pair agreed to fly out in the same plane, refusing, however, to exchange any words during the flight. Fortunately, they didn't exchange fists, either.

With time, even the way your partner slurps her tea can become annoying. Casual acquaintances are likely to be at each other's throats before the first week is out. High altitude shortens the fuse of the most even-tempered mountaineer. Climbing together extensively beforehand to learn each other's styles and idiosyncrasies is a big step toward avoiding the bitterness and frustration of failing on McKinley simply because team members find out they can't stand each other.

A group composed of people with similar levels of experience and fitness often works out best. A team of relatively inexperienced climbers can function well under the leadership of a strong climber seasoned on McKinley if the leader is willing to be patient as the others learn the ropes. An inexperienced group without good leadership can get into trouble with frightening speed. Splitting up a group high on the mountain is frequently a prelude to disaster, particularly if the group contains members of varying experience and all the strong members gather into one of the sub-groups. If the team members share a basic compatibility and the ability to communicate about grievances before they become gaping sores, they will find that climbing together on McKinley can form friendships that will last a lifetime.

Two kinds of climbers should consider hiring a guide. The first is the less experienced climber who wants to climb McKinley but who doesn't want to endure the long years of apprenticeship on lesser peaks that is required to climb McKinley safely. The second is the experienced climber who lacks local knowledge, or a partner, or who is willing to pay for the convenience of having the guides organize the equipment and pack the food. Guide services provide all group gear, saving clients the expense of buying ropes, expedition-grade tents, stoves, sleds, radios, first-aid kits and repair kits. Guide services can offer advice on what personal gear to bring and can often rent to clients the gear they lack, again saving on total expense.

Six companies are licensed by the Park Service to guide on Mt. McKinley. Their names and addresses are in Appendix A. All other guides operating on McKinley are doing so illegally. Guides operating illegally have been cited and fined by the Park Service.

Rob Dubin and Larry Palubicki approach the summit of McKinley.
Photo: Glenn Randall

Personal Equipment

I T IS PROBABLY IMPOSSIBLE for climbers on McKinley to chat for more than fifteen minutes before the conversation turns to equipment. This is for good reason: In such a harsh and unforgiving environment, everyone becomes a gear freak because their comfort, even their lives, depends on it.

Boots

Plastic double boots intended for mountaineering are the only choice for McKinley's difficult routes. They're increasingly common on easier routes as well. Leather double boots, once the universal choice for technical climbs, have essentially vanished from the market. Plastic double boots have a stiff plastic outer shell and sole that eases the strain of front-pointing on steep ice, and an inner boot made of some combination of felt, foam, polyester micro fibers, leather or vinyl. Plastic double boots weigh less than 6 pounds per pair, making them the lightest footgear normally used on McKinley. With many double boots, depending on how they're fitted, it's possible to insert an extra neoprene insole between the inner boot and the outer shell, particularly after the boots have been worn for a while and the inner boot has compressed somewhat. An extra insole adds insulation where it's most needed: directly under your foot. Plastic double boots can be stretched using the same machine boot repairmen use to stretch alpine ski boots. The boots can also be resoled.

Vapor-barrier boots, also called mouse boots, bunny boots, Korean boots and K-boots, are soft, extremely warm single boots that are useful only on the less-difficult routes. Few climbers use them these days because of the difficulty of attaching clamp-on style crampons (the preferred type), the lack of support while cramponing, and the rather amorphous fit, which allows your foot to slide back and forth inside the boot, sometimes causing blisters and hot spots. Another disadvantage is that they aren't as light as plastic boots. Although vapor-barrier boots provide a tremendous amount of insulation, they do not guarantee immunity to frostbite, as some have claimed. Dr. Peter Hackett observed four cases of toes that had become frostbitten inside vapor-barrier boots while he was researching mountain sickness on McKinley in 1982.

The preferred model of vapor-barrier boot comes with a small valve on the side to allow the air pressure inside to equalize with the pressure outside. Models that do not have a valve are not recommended for McKinley. Vapor-barrier boots are vulnerable to punctures from your own or someone else's crampons. If moisture gets inside a hole, the boot's insulating value vanishes. Also, climbers must be careful not to constrict circulation by tightening their crampon straps too tightly and compressing the flexible uppers. Clamp-on crampons must be modified before they will latch on to vapor-barrier boots.

I wore alpine-touring (also called randonnée) ski boots with extra insoles and Neoprene boot covers during my ascent of McKinley in June, 1987, because I wanted to ski as much of the descent as possible. Although not as warm as my plastic double mountaineering boots, they were adequate. Friends who wore standard alpine ski boots on the same trip had trouble with cold feet because the boots constricted circulation.

Ordinary leather single boots have no place on any McKinley route. Wearing them would almost guarantee frostbite.

Gaiters

Plastic double boots, by themselves, aren't warm enough above 14,000 feet, so insulated supergaiters or overboots are essential. Few climbers wearing vapor-barrier boots feel the need for supergaiters or overboots.

Supergaiters are knee-high gaiters that cover everything from the boot welt up. The insulated models add significant warmth, but are not as warm as overboots, which cover the entire boot including the sole. Having the sole uncovered is an advantage only on the hardest McKinley routes, some of which involve rock-climbing difficult enough that climbers must remove their crampons. Uninsulated supergaiters add little warmth and are not recommended.

Supergaiters come in two basic styles. Those with stout rubber rands grip the boot securely just above the welt and show no tendency to pop up at the toe. Supergaiters with a loop of elastic or wire running along the bottom edge of the supergaiter are a bit warmer because the insulation extends down to the sole, but have a tendency to pop up at the toe. A loop of wire crossing from right to left under the toe of the boot is sometimes necessary to keep the supergaiter toe from riding up. I sew pile fabric into the uppers of my supergaiters for still more insulation.

Overboots insulate the vulnerable sole as well as the rest of the boot, so they are highly recommended for all but the most difficult McKinley routes. They're particularly valuable during April and May, the coldest months of the normal climbing season. Crampons usually must be adjusted to a larger size to fit over overboots. Clamp-on crampons sometimes won't grip securely unless the overboots are modified by cutting a slit for the toe and heel bails.

Beware of supergaiters and overboots with snaps in regions that will be immersed in snow. Snaps, if used, usually are intended to close the zipper flap so snow stays out of the zipper. Unfortunately, they can freeze tight. On McKinley's Reality Ridge in 1982, each day's climbing ended with a monumental struggle to unsnap our supergaiters. Winning the battle usually required warming the snap with the flame of a cigarette lighter while prying with the screwdriver blade on a Swiss Army knife. Velcro-closed zipper flaps have the advantage that they can't freeze shut.

Socks

One of the best sock combinations for McKinley is a light nylon or polypropylene liner sock, worn under a coated nylon vapor-barrier sock, topped with one or more heavy socks made of wool or a blend of wool and synthetics. Vapor-barrier socks prevent evaporative heat loss and keep the insulating sock and inner boot dry. If you've never worn vapor-barrier socks before, give the concept a try by slipping a plastic bag over one foot before setting out on your next winter hike or ski-tour. You'll be astonished at the increase in warmth in the foot wearing the bag. It is absolutely essential when wearing VB socks to change liner socks and dry the VB socks every single night. If you let your feet stay wet for days, the skin will soften, blister and become susceptible to trench foot, a cold injury that can cause severe problems even though the flesh never actually freezes. Some climbers use an anti-fungal foot powder on their feet to keep the odor down and help the skin dry out.

Chris Melle at 15,000 feet on the West Buttress.
Photo: Glenn Randall

Don't start the climb with well-used socks. They're sure to develop holes quickly. Buy socks before buying your double boots, so you can fit the boots to accommodate the socks you'll actually be wearing on the mountain.

A few climbers are using neoprene skin-diver's booties or neoprene socks on McKinley. The advantages of these socks are that they are warm, function as vapor barriers and can't absorb moisture, so they dry quickly. However, snug-fitting neoprene booties probably have worsened the severity of frostbite in several cases. The neoprene used in booties is a closed-cell foam. The gas within the cells is at sea-level pressure. When these booties are taken high on McKinley, the cells, and hence the booties, expand. This action can constrict circulation inside a rigid boot shell, which can lead to wide-spread frostbite. Some boot manufacturers claim that foam inner boots can do the same thing. Although I haven't had that happen with the foam inner boots I've worn, it may be because the inner boots compressed fairly quickly with use, causing the boots to fit more loosely rather than tighter. If you do choose boots with a foam inner boot, it's probably best to fit them a bit on the large side to accommodate any potential swelling. Climbers wearing neoprene booties, like those wearing VB socks, must change their liner socks and dry their booties every night. Neoprene booties offer few advantages and create some potential danger. They are probably best avoided.

Cramming your feet into frigid, rigid boots each morning is undeniably a chore. A number of climbers, particularly those on technically demanding routes, have been seduced by the superficially attractive idea of wearing their boots to bed with them. This is an invitation to frostbite. Over a period of days, moisture builds up in your socks and boot liners, reducing their ability to insulate. The bits of snow that you inevitably drag into your sleeping bag with your boots will soon dampen your bag, reducing its insulating capability, particularly if the bag is filled with down. Whether you choose to wear vapor-barrier socks or not, you simply must remove your boots every night to dry your feet and change socks. I usually dry my socks (both liners and thick socks) by placing them inside my pile pants but outside my long underwear before I go to bed each night. Come morning, I stash the nicely dried socks in a stuff sack, ready to be donned that evening when I remove the ones that have gotten damp during the day. Whatever your footwear system, make sure you get plenty of practice with it in cold weather long before your trip. McKinley is not the place to break in boots or perfect the ideal sock combo.

Long Underwear

In recent years, a wide variety of excellent synthetic long underwear materials have become available. These new synthetics, made of polypropylene, polyester, polyvinyl chloride or a combination of polyester and nylon, absorb almost no water, so they dry quickly. Most of the new materials also wick moisture away from your skin. Unlike evaporation, wicking does not suck heat out of your body because it is driven by surface-tension forces. Wool and cotton long underwear are a poor choice for McKinley because they absorb moisture freely and dry slowly. Wet cotton is particularly lethal because the saturated fibers collapse against your skin, losing all their resiliency and hence their insulation value. Sodden cotton clings to your body, forcing perspiration to evaporate directly off your skin rather than be wicked away.

Insulating Layers

As in underwear, synthetics – polyester, nylon and polypropylene – are the materials of choice for all light and middleweight insulating layers. Synthetics absorb almost no water (less than one percent for polypropylene and polyester, about eight percent for nylon), dry extremely fast and retain their loft when wet. That doesn't mean they're warm when wet. In the words of Jack Stephenson, "Nothing is warm when wet but a hot tub." Evaporative cooling from any garment can still chill you to the marrow. However, synthetic fibers (and wool) do retain their resiliency when wet, and continue to maintain the air spaces within the garment that actually provide insulation.

Wool is inexpensive, readily available and performs adequately as an insulating layer. Its major disadvantage is that it absorbs roughly 30 percent of its weight in water, which means it dries slowly. On extended trips on McKinley, drying days may be few and far between. Once wool gets wet and heavy, it stays that way. However, wool does have a place in socks, gloves and mittens. High-quality, tightly knitted wool resists compression well, an important advantage inside a boot or when your hand is wrapped around an ice-ax or ski pole. Socks and hand wear made of yarns that blend wool with synthetic fibers also work well.

McKinley's high-altitude cold often requires four and sometimes even five layers of insulating clothing for the torso, ranging from lightweight underwear to heavyweight pile. Two pairs of heavy long johns, pile pants and wind pants usually suffice for the legs, although some people feel the need for down pants.

The same vapor-barrier principle that works well on your feet can also work well on your torso. Climbers who choose to wear a vapor-barrier shirt usually put it on over lightweight synthetic underwear. VB shirts add a lot of warmth with very little weight. They also increase freedom of movement by allowing adjacent clothing layers to slip past each other more easily. The disadvantage of VB shirts is that they require careful regulation of temperature, so you don't sweat to death. Climbers must stop to remove clothing at the first sign of overheating. However, careful regulation of sweating is a must regardless of whether you're wearing a VB shirt or not. If you are wearing one, you pay for overheating immediately, and therefore remove a layer of clothing quickly. If you aren't wearing one, it's easy to slog on until your entire inner layer is completely sweat-soaked, making it highly likely that you will become chilled when you stop.

Wind Suits

A complete wind suit (jacket and pants, jacket and bibs, or a one-piece suit) made of a waterproof/breathable material is another must. In my experience, Gore-Tex is probably still the best material, providing a high degree of waterproofness, breathability and wind-resistance. Other waterproof-breathable fabrics usually have a lower degree of water resistance, breathability, or both.

When buying a shell jacket, look for a full-coverage hood, not some skimpy design that leaves your forehead uncovered. I prefer hoods that are sewn permanently to the jacket as an integral part of the design rather than those that stow away in a pocket on the collar because I find it easier to pull an integral hood into place over my head with a gloved or mittened hand. When buying shell pants or shell bibs, consider the problem of relieving yourself during periods of intense cold and high winds. Some kind of easy-to-use drop-seat is desirable, particularly if your shell pants have suspenders. If you wear pile pants underneath, you can usually just push them down to your knees when you need to go. If your pile pants have suspenders, however, or if you're wearing pile bibs, it's convenient if they too have a drop seat that is similar in configuration to the drop seat in your shell pants. Shell bibs and pile bibs are generally warmer than shell pants and pile pants because they seal in warm air more effectively.

Parkas

Parkas can be filled with either down or synthetic fiberfill. Good down is still lighter, more compressible and more durable than the best synthetic, but 3M's new Thinsulate Lite Loft polyester/polyolefin insulation is giving lower-end down a strong run for the money. Other synthetics run a poor third. The major disadvantages of down are that it collapses when wet, takes a long time to dry and costs much more than the synthetics. A Gore-Tex shell increases the water-resistance of a down parka, but drives the price still higher. Synthetics dry fast and don't collapse when wet. On McKinley, I've rarely had a problem keeping my down jacket dry because the intense cold kept snow from melting on the jacket. Elsewhere in the Alaska Range, particularly down low during July, a synthetic parka might be a better choice.

Make sure before the trip that each layer fits over the others in the order you plan to wear them. Many size-medium people, for example, find they need a size large for their wind gear and parka. The volume of clothing required may seem ludicrous when you're trying it all on before a mirror. Bear in mind, however, that altitude dramatically increases the problem of staying warm. Being outside when it's zero degrees at sea-level is nothing like being outside at the same temperature at 20,000 feet.

Pockets are in endless demand on McKinley as storage places for your film, pocket knife, cigarette lighter, lip balm, sunscreen, extra twist-ties, radio batteries (which must be warm to function when inserted into the radio) and a host of other miscellaneous essentials. Look for zipper-closed pockets in both your shell gear and your insulating layers. Be sure that the contents of those pockets won't be trapped beneath your pack waist belt or harness. Pockets that close with Velcro are a nuisance because the Velcro grabs your gloves when you try to reach inside.

Full-length zippers along the outsides of both your wind pants and pile pants are a blessing because they allow you to ventilate without stopping to strip clothing, and because they let you add or subtract clothing without removing your boots. Full-length separating zippers on your wind pants let you put them on without removing your crampons or skis.

Gloves and Mittens

McKinley's upper regions are frequently cold enough that you need to layer your hand protection just as you layer your torso and legs. I usually carry a couple of pairs of lightweight knitted polypropylene or polyester gloves for warm days, and for time spent reading and cooking in the tent. These dry fast but often have a lifetime of less than one expedition. Don't start with used liner gloves. You'll have holes in them within a week. An alternative is to carry a couple of pairs of lightweight cross-country gloves with leather palms and fingers and a knitted back. Although more expensive, they last longer than lightweight knitted gloves and don't get wet quite as fast.

As the temperature drops, I add a pair of pile-lined, nylon-shelled mittens over my liner gloves. After wearing out a brand-new pair of nylon overmitts in less than nine days on Mt. Hunter, and severely frostbiting my fingers, I've learned to carry a backup pair. Make sure the liners are removable for quicker drying inside your sleeping bag at night.

For still colder conditions, I substitute a pair of heavy wool gloves for the lightweight liner gloves, then don the pile-lined mitten shells. For extreme cold, I also carry a pair of heavy wool mittens that will fit inside my pile-lined shell mittens. I always wear idiot strings to keep my mitten shells from departing for Fairbanks at inopportune moments.

Head Gear

In addition to an ordinary wool or synthetic ski hat for days of moderate temperatures, you should bring a full balaclava to take the sting out of colder days. Several companies make lightweight synthetic balaclavas that can be layered beneath a heavier one. For many years I've enjoyed a garment I sewed up myself consisting of a lightweight polypropylene balaclava sewn to a polypropylene long underwear shirt. To ventilate, I added a long zipper that runs from chin to sternum. Essentially, I created a hooded polypropylene sweatshirt. Combining a neck gaiter with a hat is an adequate substitute for a balaclava. Of late, I've become partial to a pile-lined, Gore-Tex shelled hat that not only keeps my head dry and warm in snowstorms, but stays dry itself, unlike a knitted ski hat worn without a hood.

Silk or polypropylene face masks help cut the wind, but aren't as effective as neoprene face masks that cover the lower half of the face. For complete protection, face masks must be worn with ski goggles. Although goggles are prone to freeze up, they can change agony into comfort when facing a blizzard. You also can use goggles instead of sunglasses during windy but clear conditions to keep the skin around your eyes warm. Make sure goggles have amber lenses that block UV. Double-paned goggles are typically more brittle but less prone to fogging than single-paned ones. Both a face mask and goggles with amber lenses should be considered essential.

Quality mountaineering sunglasses designed for high-altitude must be worn to prevent snow-blindness. They should block at least 90 percent of incoming ultraviolet light. A spare pair can come in handy. A leather nose guard attached to the bridge of your glasses makes it much easier to keep your nose from peeling like a banana. Duct tape from your repair kit can be fashioned into a less elegant substitute for a leather nose guard. And, after the trip, you can walk into a drugstore, ask for a tube of lip sunscreen and tell them to put it on your bill.

Sleeping Bags

The same synthetics versus down argument that applies to parkas also applies to sleeping bags, except that the actual difference in weight and bulk is even more significant.

Camp at 14,300 feet on the West Buttress. The ski tracks mark Blind Faith.
Photo: Glenn Randall

A good vapor-barrier sleeping bag liner with sealed seams helps keep a down bag dry. Used while wearing the proper amount of clothing, a VB liner lets you sleep comfortably in temperatures 10 degrees colder than you could without one. By leaving the liner open at the neck, some moisture can escape, yet your bag remains dry. Sealing the liner at the neck definitely raises both the humidity and the temperature inside. Misusing a VB liner will make you feel you're sweltering in tropical Borneo instead of camping on a subarctic mountain. I regard a VB liner as an essential part of a down bag. It's equally important that the bag either have a Gore-Tex shell or that you carry a separate Gore-Tex sleeping bag cover for it.

Even the best VB liners allow a slight amount of moisture to build up in your bag during long storms. Spending a few hours drying gear after a long spell of bad weather is often worth the time. Synthetic sleeping bags don't require VB liners, of course, but a liner does add significant warmth.

As in parkas, the best synthetic in terms of warmth-to-weight ratio and compressibility is currently 3M's Lite Loft. The difference between the best synthetic bag and an average down bag grows smaller every year. If saving weight and pack space are important and you're willing to pay down's price and invest the energy required to keep it dry on the mountain, down is probably the best bet. If pack space and weight are not as critical, while price is, go with a synthetic. West Buttress climbers can get away with a bit more weight than climbers on highly technical routes on the South Face.

Mountaineers in every month of the normal climbing season can expect to experience nighttime temperatures of −30 and −40 degrees F at their high camp. Choose a sleeping bag rated to −30 degrees F, unless you know from experience that you can get away with something lighter. Sleeping metabolisms and the amount of insulation people require differ. Camping out in the cold on an extended trip is the best way to determine how hefty a bag and how much clothing you need. Make sure your bag is big enough for you to wear enough clothing and still have room for your camera and water bottle. Too big a bag, however, is excessively heavy and not as warm because of the "pumping effect." A loose-fitting bag allows air to circulate freely inside the bag as you toss and turn. That sets up heat-robbing convection currents and also tends to pump warm air out of the mouth of the bag.

Foam Pads

Be sure your sleeping pad won't become brittle in extreme cold. Old Ensolite pads, for example, turn into fence slats if you try to roll them in sub-zero weather. At least half-inch of insulation is required, and many people find that carrying two ⅜-inch pads is worth the weight. To prevent the pads from wandering during the night, I usually glue the two pads together at one end. Don't glue them along the full length, or you won't be able to roll them compactly. Ordinary air mattresses are too heavy, too vulnerable to puncture and permit too much heat flow through convection to be useful. Therm-a-Rests are lighter, provide a wonderful night's sleep and don't allow convection because they are filled with open-cell foam. They're still vulnerable to puncture, however, particularly if you play mumblety-peg nearby, as a friend of mine did at Kahiltna Base just before starting up the West Buttress. A combination of a Therm-a-Rest and a foam pad is very comfortable and safe, with no risk of losing all your sleeping-pad insulation if your Therm-a-Rest does spring a leak.

Various companies now sell lightweight, legless chairs that are made of nylon and aluminum or carbon-fiber stays. Some contain their own closed-cell foam padding; others are designed to serve as a framework for your sleeping pad. These may seem like a luxury that only decadent backpackers could afford to carry. However, McKinley climbers spend an awful lot of time sitting around melting water. A comfortable chair makes the process a whole lot less tedious. Chairs are worth their weight on routes like the West Buttress and Muldrow.

For a more complete harangue on the art of staying warm, see my book *Cold Comfort,* published by Lyons & Burford.

Ice Tools

On easier routes, the ice ax serves mostly as a walking stick and as a tool for self-arrest, so it should be longer than 60 cm for most people. If your only ax is 60 cm or shorter and you don't want to buy another, consider carrying ski poles for glacier travel and only using the ax on steeper terrain up high. Don't make the mistake of carrying only ski poles for the entire route. Falls without an ice ax to self-arrest have been fatal, even on the West Buttress.

The deeply rotten ice and fluted, corniced ridge crests common on difficult Alaskan routes demand slightly different tools than do vertical frozen waterfalls. The major difference is that, in Alaska, two long-handled tools (45 to 60 cm), with spikes on the ends of both, give greater security when plunging the shafts into crumbling snow/ice. Using replaceable-pick tools and carrying a spare pick provides an extra margin of safety on difficult routes.

Ice tools should be tied to your harness regardless of the route's difficulty. They can be lost even on a level glacier if you take a fall into a crevasse.

Crampons

Flexible crampons work fine on routes like the Muldrow and West Buttress. They're also the lightest crampons around and among the most durable. Rigid crampons are preferable for routes with sustained, steep ice. Crampons have been known to break at awkward times – like in the middle of a 50-degree ice slope at sunset in a howling gale, as happened to me on Mt. Hunter. Some crampons, particularly Footfangs, are modular enough to be easily repairable in the field if you carry spare parts. If you don't bring Footfangs, either consider bringing a spare pair of crampons or think very seriously about the consequences if your only pair should break. Clamp-on crampons are infinitely superior to strap-on models because they go on fast and don't have straps that can constrict circulation and encourage frostbite.

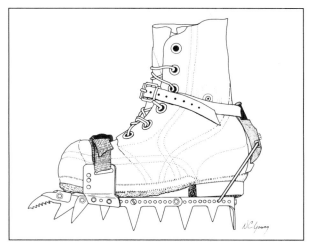

Footfangs (shown here modified for use with bunny boots).
Drawing: Nancy Young

Harnesses

As late as 1967, some mountaineers still ventured onto Alaska's heavily crevassed glaciers with the rope simply knotted around their waist, a foolhardy practice that could easily have cost someone his life. A full sit harness is a prerequisite for safe glacier travel. Many climbers also wear a chest harness, an excellent additional precaution for those carrying a heavy pack. On McKinley, that includes almost everybody almost all the time. Falling into a crevasse laden with a big pack will probably leave you dangling upside down if you're not wearing a chest harness. Righting yourself, then prusiking out, is far more difficult than you can imagine if you've never done it before. Chest harnesses do make changing clothes more time-consuming, but everyone who has taken a bad crevasse fall will agree that it's a small price to pay.

If you look around, you should be able to find a harness that will allow you to stay tied in to the waist belt while dropping the leg loops to relieve yourself. Such a harness saves lots of time and aggravation, particularly on technical routes. Seemingly minor details like this make a major difference in enjoyment on the mountain. If you can find one, a harness that does not require stepping through the leg loops is convenient because the harness can be put on and removed without removing crampons.

Packs

Most McKinley climbers choose internal-frame packs because they ride tighter to the body and have a lower center of gravity than external-frame packs, and because they flex a bit as you move. All these characteristics make internal-frame packs easier to balance than external frames while skiing and climbing. However, any number of climbers have reached the summit of McKinley via the less difficult routes with external-frame packs on their backs. A large-capacity pack bag is essential; external pockets, many lash-on points and plenty of accessory straps are useful. Make sure you've carried substantial weight in the pack on a multi-day trip before attempting McKinley. Ill-fitting packs, carried for day after day, aggravate the back fatigue and pain common with even the best-fitting packs. Women, in particular, should be sure the pack bag doesn't ride too low; many women have trouble with packs designed for the longer male torso. One woman I know spent five hours at 14,300 feet altering the harness of her pack with a Speedy Stitcher because the pain had become intolerable.

Skis and Snowshoes

During periods of settled weather, the West Buttress trail becomes so packed that some climbers walk it in boots alone, foolishly disregarding the additional protection against crevasse falls provided by using skis or snowshoes. In early season and during stormy weather, skis or snowshoes are essential, even on the West Buttress. On other routes, you'll probably use them constantly. All expedition members should bring one or the other, regardless of the route chosen.

Skiers should consider the consequences if they twist a knee or break a leg while trying to cut up some powder run. Unless you're an expert skier, you'll probably find that traveling on snowshoes is safer. On the down side, snowshoes aren't quite as effective as skis in bridging crevasses. Skis are faster and more fun than snowshoes, but demand an equally high level of proficiency from all team members, as skiers, like everyone else, should always travel roped together. It's all too easy to get excited about the skiing and neglect to notice that you've allowed 50 feet of slack to accumulate in the rope. Huge packs and sleds magnify the problem of keeping the rope taut. Although many people ski the Kahiltna unroped, the practice is not recommended. Every year people get cocky about their ability to judge hidden crevasses. Almost every year, someone has a serious accident as a result.

Sleds

Flat-bottomed plastic children's sleds (not the kind with runners) take a load off your back and make ferrying supplies on the glacier much easier. Climbers usually attach themselves to the sled with a pair of traces made of polypropylene rope or nylon webbing. The traces run from the front corners of the sled to your harness or pack, where they are clipped in with a carabiner. Beware of attaching a sled to your pack's ice-ax loops. These loops are not usually designed to withstand that kind of load. In many places on McKinley's glaciers, a sled that rips loose could be lost forever into a crevasse or over a cliff.

Sleds, while undeniably useful, have the temperament of a mule. If loaded too heavily on a traverse, they frequently roll, dumping their contents in the snow. Putting everything into a duffel bag, then lashing the duffel bag onto the sled can help. Transferring some weight to your pack so the sled is less top-heavy is another remedy. While going downhill, children's sleds tend to overrun you and clip you in the heels. Running a bungee cord across the bottom of the sled at right angles to the direction of travel creates friction that usually reduces the number of times the sled kicks your legs out from under you. A second alternative is to run the nylon traces through six-foot lengths of one-inch diameter PVC pipe. A final solution, for those in the middle or at the front of the rope, is to clip the back of the sled into a figure-eight knot in the climbing rope. The climber behind you can then keep the sled off your heels by keeping the rope taut. This solution also keeps the sled from striking you if you go into a crevasse and it goes in with you. I'll have more to say on this subject in the chapter on Campcraft and Glacier Travel.

The final problem with sleds is that most climbing harnesses make poor hauling harnesses. They frequently chafe and pinch, even through many layers of clothing. Padding the harness with spare gloves or mittens helps. Expensive high-density polyethylene or fiberglass sleds have rigid traces that connect the sled to a padded hauling harness. The harness provides comfort, while the rigid traces reduce rolling and keep the sled from blind-siding you when you're going downhill.

Some climbers prefer to haul loads in a drag bag, essentially a duffel bag attached to the hauling line with a swivel. The bag can be covered with a plastic tube tent to reduce friction. Drag bags roll freely on side hills without hindering you. They're also less prone to overrunning you because they don't slide quite as easily on the snow. Don't make the mistake of assuming a big plastic barrel will substitute for a drag bag. Barrels roll a little too freely side-to-side. In 1987, I watched a climber who was towing a barrel just barely prevent her rebellious load from rolling into the giant slit latrine at Kahiltna Base.

Miscellaneous Essentials

Either ascenders or prusiks are necessary for getting yourself out of a crevasse and as a self-belay while climbing beside a fixed line. If you bring ascenders, choose a model with a large handle that you can grab easily while wearing mittens. Gibbs ascenders have the advantage that the climber's weight forces the cam into the rope, which causes them to grip better than conventional ascenders if the rope is icy. Conventional ascenders use a spring to force the cam into the rope, so the camming action is not as forceful. Prusik knots are inconvenient on a fixed line because you must constantly tie and untie the prusik knot. They're certainly lighter, however, and some people feel they grip better on an icy rope than conventional ascenders. All ascenders must have foot slings attached. There should also be a sling from each ascender to your harness. If you're unfamiliar with your ascenders, practice climbing a rope with them before the trip.

Water bottles should have wide mouths (to reduce spills when filling them) and should be insulated. That won't prevent them from freezing; it will just slow down the rate at which they freeze. Thermoses are better yet, but heavy; some are fragile and have too limited a capacity.

Headlamps are needed only for early-season ascents. Lithium batteries work even in severe cold. Ordinary batteries must be kept warm, a nuisance because of the great number of other items that also require warmth. See the chapter on McKinley's climate for more details on hours of daylight.

If you're approaching from the north in late May or June, bring a mosquito headnet and plenty of mosquito repellent.

A good book can make a storm day refreshing instead of a bore. Some people choose intellectually demanding reading on the theory that the concentration required to plow through such weighty stuff takes their minds off the imminent danger of their tent blowing away with them in it. Others, seeking the same escape, choose fast-paced action novels full of sex, drugs and violence. Reading about the incredible hardships of early mountaineers and polar explorers can make your own plight seem trivial. A journal to record trials and tribulations makes great reading in the years afterwards. There's so much traffic on the West Buttress that it's quite feasible to write letters to friends and loved ones, then send them out with expeditions heading downhill. In most cases, they actually arrive before you get home. Consider bringing some stamped envelopes, writing paper, a pen or pencil and a list of addresses of people you'd like to startle with a letter mailed from 14,300 feet on the highest mountain in North America.

As you assemble the enormous pile of gear you need for McKinley, consider ways you can tweak it to allow you to do as much as possible with your gloves on. In the relatively mild winter temperatures of the Lower 48, you usually can get away with performing a few operations with bare hands. On McKinley, particularly as the days go by and your hands get raw and sensitive to the cold, you'll find that taking your gloves off to do anything is increasingly irritating. Most people who spend a lot of time outdoors in the winter know how useful it is to tie small loops of stout cord (I like 4 mm perlon) through all of the zipper pulls on their shell clothing, tent, sleeping bag, pack, etc. These zipper pulls let you manipulate your zippers with gloves on. Apply the same logic to other items of gear. For example, my assistant guide in 1984 had just bought a new pack. The accessory straps on the pack lid turned out to be just barely long enough to reach around her double foam pads.

To attach her foam pads using the stock straps, she needed to unthread, then rethread the ladder buckles each time, which meant she needed to remove her gloves. That's a trivial matter on a ski trip in Colorado, but when repeated 25 times during the course of an Alaskan expedition, it becomes a real annoyance. Replacing the stock straps with longer ones would have saved her a lot of grief because she could have loosened the straps without unthreading them, then slid the rolled foam pads into the loops and tightened the straps. Another example: The Stephenson Warmlite tents I've used on some expeditions are rather awkward to pitch with gloves on. By drilling a hole through the end of the pole, then tying a loop of cord through the hole, I gave myself a convenient handle that I could use, even with gloves on, to lever the end of the pole into the pole sleeve. As you examine your gear closely, I'm sure you'll find other ways to modify it to make it as convenient to use as possible.

Chris Melle, Rob Dubin and Dale Atkins ferry loads at 12,000 feet on the West Buttress.
Photo: Glenn Randall

Sunset on Mt. Hunter from 14,300 feet on McKinley.
Photo: Glenn Randall

Group Gear

GROUP GEAR – tents, stoves, ropes, wands, snow shovels, etc. – includes all the gear that everybody uses, but nobody throws into his pack without first making sure that his partner is taking a fair share.

Tents

No tent light enough to carry can be relied upon to stand up, unprotected, in the worst winds that McKinley can fling at you. Some climbers on the West Buttress and Muldrow dispense with tents altogether and simply dig snow caves or build igloos at every camp. Igloos and caves certainly come highly recommended in severe storms. Most McKinley climbers, however, find that the warmth and light inside a tent, even under hazy skies, lifts morale and helps dry gear. Expeditions usually bring both a tent and the means to build snow shelters.

Dome tents with either three or four interlacing poles offer about as much security as a reasonably portable tent can offer. The poles support each other, and the smooth aerodynamic arc of the roof makes the tent wind resistant. The tents are strongest when pitched on a level tent platform and when the corners are staked out. Most McKinley climbers use a dome tent of one kind or another. The tents typically weigh from 7 to 11 pounds for the two- and three-person versions. Any tent you choose should be billed as a four-season model. Don't start up McKinley with a well-worn tent. If a bad windstorm catches you unprepared, you could end up with a pack full of tattered nylon and broken aluminum as you hightail it for base camp.

Pitching any tent with a shock-corded pole can be a real problem in severe cold when the shock cords inside the poles lose their elasticity and don't allow the pole sections to be fitted together. Rubbing the pole hard and fast with a mittened hand will usually warm it enough to allow the tent to be pitched. Pulling repeatedly on the shock cord itself can also do the trick. As a last resort, of course, the shock cord can be cut, but I've never seen a case where that was necessary.

Stoves

A good stove is even more important than a good tent. Without a stove, there is no water to drink. Without four to five quarts of water per day, a climber on McKinley quickly becomes severely dehydrated. Dehydration predisposes a climber to altitude illness, frostbite, hypothermia and shock following even minor injury. At least one expedition I know of has had to turn back because the one stove they had failed and could not be repaired. Any stove can break, clog or be damaged in a fall or through being dropped. A complete repair kit and a backup stove provide peace of mind.

A climber should practice using his/her stove before the trip, under all conditions, to learn its idiosyncrasies – like what makes it flare and whether it can leak fuel. Such problems are even more serious on McKinley than elsewhere because the weather is bad enough that most teams find they must cook in a tent at least once in a while, despite the clear danger of fire and carbon monoxide (CO) poisoning. Two experienced Swiss climbers died at 14,300 feet on the West Buttress in 1986 from carbon monoxide poisoning caused by cooking in an unventilated tent. Carbon monoxide poisoning may also have contributed to many cases of altitude illness. The symptoms are similar: headache, dizziness and nausea. If you must cook in your tent, adequate ventilation is absolutely vital. For many tents, that means cooking with the door largely open. If you can't feel the cold blasts of wind on your face, you know CO can't get out. Don't heat a tent with a stove.

When cooking in a snowcave or igloo, punch a hole the diameter of a ski-pole basket in the roof directly above the stove. The hole can be plugged with a snow block when you're not cooking. Igloos and snowcaves become ice-glazed after several days of use. The glaze tightly seals the walls, increasing the threat of carbon monoxide poisoning and thus the necessity for plenty of fresh air. The effects of CO and altitude hypoxia appear to be additive, which makes CO exposure at altitude more dangerous than at sea-level.

A recent study on McKinley found that CO production increased significantly if water condensed on the cooking pot and dripped onto the burner, dampening the flame. Let the water in the pot warm up, then add snow slowly, so the pot itself stays warm, reducing condensation.

If you should come across a conscious victim of CO poisoning, (your friends in a nearby tent, for example) first shut off the stove, if it's still running, then have the victim hyperventilate in fresh air. If the victim is comatose, administer oxygen if it's available, or force the victim to hyperventilate by giving mouth-to-mouth artificial respiration. If the victim doesn't regain consciousness within a few minutes, you're in big trouble. Evacuate the victim to a lower altitude immediately.

White-gas stoves such as those made by MSR and Coleman burn hot and use the same fuel that almost every climber uses, so if you run out on the mountain you may be able to find someone with some fuel to spare. The fuel is cheap and readily available in stores. Repair of white gas stoves, if required, usually is a simple matter of replacing gaskets or o-rings. MSR, in particular, has gone to great lengths to make their stoves easy to maintain in the field – an important characteristic on McKinley. Beware of white-gas stoves that don't have a pump. These can be hard to keep working in the cold.

Almost all white-gas stoves require priming. If over-primed, all of them can flare up and singe your eyebrows or worse. Using priming paste or alcohol reduces the flare-up problem but doesn't eliminate the possibility of spills while filling the stove's fuel tank. It's a good idea to fill stoves and cook outside the tent whenever possible. Accidentally igniting a pool of spilled gas inside a tent would be a disaster. Fuel containers and stoves must be kept separate from food. The manufacturer of MSR stoves says that in severe cold (below -10 degrees F) the fuel bottle for the MSR XG-K II must be warmed to about zero to prevent wax impurities in the fuel from precipitating and clogging the fuel line. Used with the proper precautions, however, a white-gas stove with a pump will serve you well.

Kerosene stoves burn a less volatile fuel, which makes handling the stoves and fuel safer, but the fumes are even worse than those from white gas. Kerosene is also a dirty fuel, which means the stove's orifice requires regular cleaning. Kerosene is an uncommon fuel on McKinley, so be sure you don't run out.

Any lighted stove set down in the snow without some form of insulation will melt into the snow, usually unevenly, and tip over unless caught in time. The consequences range from losing dinner to igniting any flammable material nearby. MSRs, in particular, can burn so hot they will melt ordinary foam pads if used as insulation. A snow shovel performs adequately as a stove support, although it too will melt into the snow eventually. A small square of plywood works better, and is probably worth the weight on the Muldrow or West Buttress routes. However, if you over-prime the stove and spill gas onto the plywood, the plywood will ignite. Try covering the plywood with a piece of sheet metal, such as a metal "for sale" sign or something similar.

Another solution to the stove problem is to modify a butane cartridge stove, like the Bleuet 206. Butane is a cleaner fuel than white gas or kerosene, so butane stoves have few clogging problems. Butane cartridges can't contaminate food. The stove burns quietly and the flare-up danger is less, though not entirely absent. Flare-ups can occur if the stove is lit soon after it has been shaken, because liquid fuel droplets are mixed in with the gas. Allowing the stove to sit quietly for a minute or two before lighting reduces this problem. Always light the stove with the valve just barely open. The fumes from burning butane are less obnoxious than those from white gas or kerosene, but the tent must still be well ventilated. MSR's data shows that their Rapidfire butane stove produces the least carbon monoxide of all the stoves in their line. The XG-K and Whisperlite, when burning white gas, produce somewhat more carbon monoxide. Burning kerosene in an XG-K or Whisperlite produces the most. The Bleuet 206 is very simple, with only a few moving parts. Bleuet stoves are not immune to breakdown, but they are much more resistant than more complicated white gas and kerosene stoves.

Butane stoves only work if the cartridge is warm enough for the pressurized butane inside to vaporize. Normal butane liquefies at 31 degrees F. Unmodified stoves burning normal butane produce practically no heat below that temperature because nearly all of the butane is in liquid form; the remaining gaseous butane exerts such a low pressure that very little flows out of the burner when the valve is opened. Fortunately, cartridges are now available for the Bleuet that burn a mixture of propane and butane. Propane liquefies at -44 degrees F, so the combined fuel works much better than normal butane in severe cold. MSR and other manufacturers offer stoves that burn iso-butane, a variety of butane that liquefies at 11 degrees F. This fuel also works better in the cold than normal butane. High altitude, with its lower air pressure, increases the output of butane stoves compared to their performance at sea-level. Just as water boils at a lower temperature as you go higher, so too do butane and its variants. The lower boiling point means higher pressure in the cartridge, which increases the amount of gas flowing out of the burner, and hence the heat output of the stove. As I've experienced firsthand, you'll get much better performance at 14,300 feet on McKinley at zero degrees, for example, than you will during a January cold snap in Arches National Park.

On McKinley, a butane stove, no matter what fuel you're using, is nearly worthless unless it's used in combination with a hanging pot setup. Setting the butane cartridge in the snow guarantees low output. By converting the lower pot of a double boiler into a windscreen from which the stove hangs, using the upper pot for cooking, and hanging the whole affair from the tent roof, several problems are solved. The pot is resistant to spills. The stove can't melt into the floor and tip over. Also, the stove is insulated from the cold floor, so it burns more efficiently. Off and on, various manufacturers have offered hanging cook sets for various butane stoves. They're also relatively easy to make yourself from an inexpensive aluminum double boiler.

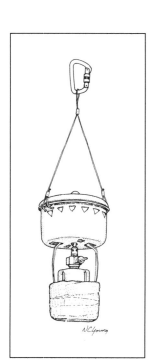

Modified butane hanging stove.
Drawing: Nancy Young

Before starting a butane stove, the cartridge should be pre-warmed with body heat. To keep the stove running, the hanging cook set system can be modified further by insulating the cartridge with closed-cell foam. A few climbers have further modified their stoves by running copper tubing from the flame area to the cartridge. The copper tubing conducts heat to the cartridge, enhancing heat output. Sounds dangerous, since overheating the cartridge could cause it to explode. If you try this, be extremely careful.

Despite your best efforts, you probably won't get as much heat from a butane stove as you will from a white-gas stove. To my mind, the butane stove's convenience and safety makes up for the longer wait to get that first hot drink inside me. If you plan to bring a butane stove, experiment beforehand in cold weather to learn what to expect. The second major disadvantage of the system is the cost of the cartridges, which exceeds that of white gas and kerosene by a factor of five. In addition, all those empty cartridges must be carried off the mountain.

White-gas and kerosene stoves burn a minimum of ½ cup of fuel per person per day. Bleuet stoves burn a minimum of ⅓ of a cartridge per person per day. These figures assume you're using instant foods requiring only the addition of hot water. Actually cooking foods, such as macaroni or rice, could increase these fuel requirements by 20 or 30 percent. With any stove, carry a 25-percent margin above your basic estimate of fuel needs. Stretching food is easy; stretching fuel is not. For white gas stoves, carrying one quart of fuel per day for a four-person team will give you a comfortable safety margin. Most expeditions find they have extra fuel. Don't leave it behind on the mountain using the excuse that "someone in an emergency" will need it. In the last few years, tremendous amounts of excess fuel have accumulated on McKinley. Excess fuel, like abandoned food caches, simply becomes litter. Pack out all your excess fuel.

Expeditions should bring at least one stove for every three people. Melting enough water is a very time-consuming task, regardless of the number of stoves. Bringing one stove for every two people, particularly if you're using butane stoves, saves time and helps ensure that fatigue doesn't discourage climbers from melting as much water as they really need.

In 1992, the only fuel available in Talkeetna was white gas. Pilots generally fly gallons of white gas in to Kahiltna Base in advance. Climbers pay for the white gas they'll need when they pay their pilot for the flight, then pick up the white gas after they land on the glacier. It's illegal to fly with butane cartridges in your luggage, so climbers arriving in Anchorage by air will have to buy cartridges there. Check in advance to make sure the store you'll be shopping at has as much as you'll need. Addresses for Anchorage outdoor equipment shops are in Appendix A. If you're using a kerosene stove, you'll have to buy your kerosene in Anchorage as well. Stove fuel is not allowed on the Alaska Railroad, so if you buy fuel in Anchorage, you'll have to hire a shuttle service to get from Anchorage to Talkeetna. See Appendix A for addresses.

Ropes

Most McKinley climbers use 9 mm ropes treated for water repellency. For recommendations on the length of rope that should be used by teams of different sizes, see the chapter on Campcraft and Glacier Travel.

Fixed ropes are no longer commonly used on McKinley. Any fixed rope used must be removed completely after the climb. In the heady exhaustion of victory, however, few climbers actually manage to remove their ropes. Rockfall, wind and the melting out of anchors quickly make abandoned fixed ropes untrustworthy. The result can mirror what happened to the Cassin in the '60s and '70s. Each successive party fixed their own rope. In some places, as many as a dozen useless and ugly fixed ropes lay side by side. Unwary mountaineers who trusted an old fixed rope have been killed when it broke unexpectedly. Climbers contemplating a route they feel will require fixed rope should consider an alpine-style ascent of a technically easier route. The challenge will be the same, and the beauty of both routes will be preserved. Fortunately for the Cassin, the number of abandoned fixed ropes is gradually decreasing, as wind and passing climbers cut them away.

One section of the West Buttress, from 15,000 to 16,000 feet, commonly does have fixed rope on it. The guides on an early-season ascent usually fix a new rope there each year, then leave it for later parties. The rope should be trusted – grudgingly – only after a hearty yank on each section.

Wands

Bamboo garden stakes with short strips of bright-colored surveyor's tape tied or glued to the ends make good wands for marking the route. Travel on both the West Buttress and the Muldrow can be extremely confusing at almost every elevation, including, most importantly, the summit dome above Denali Pass. Glacier travel on other routes can be equally confusing. Wands should be placed every rope length so that if a severe whiteout descends during the return trip, the climber at the end of the rope can remain at the last known wand while the leader looks for the next one.

Wands also are useful for marking caches. Caches should be marked with several double-length wands (two wands taped together). Write your name and date on the surveyor's tape so you recognize which cache is yours.

Traffic on the West Buttress is heavy enough that many climbers assume someone else will have already wanded the route. The truth is that most of the route will have some wands, but the sequence of wands is likely to have large gaps in it. An individual wand rarely remains standing for more than a week or two. One day in June, 1987, five friends and I were making a carry at about 8,000 feet on the West Buttress when a storm rolled in. The range of visibility began dropping quickly. We had not brought many wands, assuming incorrectly that the route would be well-wanded. But the route back to our camp was poorly marked, so we turned around before reaching our goal for the day and hustled back to camp as the whiteout intensified and snowfall obliterated our tracks. The next morning, we saw a team of a half-dozen climbers plod wearily over a nearby rise. They had pushed on into the storm while carrying a load. When finding their camp again proved to be impossible, they were forced to dig a snowcave and bivouac in what they were wearing, a debilitating, demoralizing and unnecessary ordeal.

Even on the West Buttress, climbers should always bring 30 or 40 wands to fill in the gaps where wands have blown down or melted out and fallen over. Groups trying the West Buttress in early season, before the trail is wanded by other parties, might well use 75 or 100 wands. As a general rule, it's okay on the West Buttress to leave in place the wands you set to mark the route because other parties assume some wands will be in place (if everyone brought enough wands to mark the entire route, the glacier would look like a dayglo Bonsai forest). However, wands marking your caches or your campsite should be removed and carried off the mountain. On all other routes, wands left behind simply become litter. Climbers ferrying loads on other routes should clean their wands during their last carry over each section, particularly if they are planning to descend by another route.

Other Group Gear

Snow shovels are vital for snow-caving, wall-building and latrine-digging. Large, aluminum-bladed grain scoops are perfect. They're easier to carry if you shorten the blade and handle. Small, stout, aluminum-bladed avalanche shovels, the kind carried by backcountry skiers, also work well, particularly in hard snow. Plastic-bladed avalanche shovels are too flimsy for serious digging.

Building a snow wall to protect your tent from high winds is an essential part of establishing a McKinley camp. It's far easier to erect a wall by stacking snow blocks than by piling up snow. Snow saws make block walls a cinch. They're also essential for igloo-building.

The repair kit should include needles of assorted sizes, sewing thread, Speedy

Stitcher with extra needles and extra-strong thread, darning needle, yarn, wire, duct tape, spare parts for stoves, ski bindings, crampons and ice tools, any special wrenches or other tools required for repairing equipment, small pair of vise grips or pliers and 100 feet of strong cord. Pay serious attention to packing your repair kit. You'll need it more often than you think. Examine each piece of equipment in advance and plan what to do if some part of it breaks.

The best map and the best photographs of the McKinley area come from Bradford Washburn's pioneering work in the '40s and '50s. The map is available from many mountaineering stores and from the University of Alaska Press. Washburn's photos are available from Boston's Museum of Science. The addresses and phone numbers are in Appendix A.

A thermometer will satisfy that burning curiosity to know just how freezing cold it really is. Maximum-minimum thermometers tell you how cold it actually was when it was way too cold to even think of getting out of your sleeping bag.

Before the trip, scrutinize each piece of personal and group equipment for any sign of wear and tear. One expedition on McKinley puts the equivalent of a year's normal use on every stitch, buckle, zipper, bolt and scrap of metal. Don't start a trip with well-used gear. Brand-new gear can be almost as much of a liability as heavily used gear. Every item of equipment should be purchased months ahead of time and tested thoroughly. McKinley is no place to discover manufacturing defects in brand-new gear, or that old gear was closer to its grave than you thought.

So many items of group and personal gear are required to climb McKinley that hardly anyone can remember them all. Typically, too, there are a thousand miscellaneous tasks that must be completed before the expedition. Create a checklist like the sample list in Appendix B, then make sure everything is checked off before you start the trip. That should prevent arrival on the glacier without something crucial, like the matches to light the stove or the fuel to burn in it. One companion on my first trip to Alaska felt so strongly about the need to write down every task that he started one list with the command, "Find main list."

Dale Atkins and Chris Melle rest at 16,600 feet on the West Buttress.
Photo: Glenn Randall

Food

PEOPLE WHO HAVE NEVER done a wilderness trip longer than a few days often pack food using the eyeball method: if it looks like the right amount, bring it. Most of the time, people bring too much. That's fine for a short trip, where an extra pound or two of food scarcely matters, but on McKinley the eyeball method can make your load-carrying days very long and your temper very short.

Some people pack food by volume, bringing, let's say, one cup of cereal for breakfast each morning. Unfortunately, that can easily lead to a fairly large difference in the actual number of calories in each meal, because food differs in density. To make each breakfast equally satisfying, for example, you might need to bring 1¼ cups of granola, but only one cup of Grape-Nuts because granola is less dense than Grape-Nuts. To my mind, sorting out how much to bring of each item on the basis of volume is unnecessarily complicated.

The best method, in my organization-obsessed opinion, is to weigh out your food. Instead of bringing a different volume of cereal for each breakfast, for example, you can simply decide that you need five ounces each morning, and bring that. I use an inexpensive postage scale to weigh out each bag of food.

Weighing out your food presupposes that you know how much you eat in terms of ounces. Few people do; I didn't until I started weighing out food for my first backpacking trips, then compared what I actually ate to the number of ounces I'd brought. The problem is compounded by the fact that so many of the foods people eat at home – fruit, sauces, meat, many vegetables, everything canned – are already saturated with water. On the mountain, however, almost everything is dry. A food's dry weight bears little relation to its cooked weight. A typical Mountain House freeze-dried dinner, for example, weighs about 4 ounces dry, 16 ounces after rehydration. It's easy to look at a day's worth of dried food and think that it can't possibly be enough, because you're comparing it to the volume of water-saturated food you normally eat at home.

Start food planning for McKinley by deciding the total number of ounces to bring per person per day. If you're new to thinking in terms of ounces, you'll need to pack a few days of food by the ounce and complete a multi-day ski-tour or snowshoe trip before the climb. That should give you a good idea of your personal needs when working hard in cold weather. How much food each person requires per day varies greatly. Sex, height, build, metabolism, level of activity and temperature all affect the amount a person needs. My metabolism (I'm 5'8", 135 pounds) seems to require between 28 and 32 ounces per day. For alpine-style climbs of technically difficult routes where weight is critical, I bring 28 ounces per day and expect to be a bit hungry on long days. For less demanding climbs, I bring 32 ounces a day and expect to have a little bit of food left over on the easy days. That gradually accumulating surplus provides a reserve for very long days, or an extra day if the climb takes a bit longer than expected. Remember that any extra food must be carried off the mountain, not cached on the pretext that other climbers will use it. Abandoned food caches almost invariably become trash heaps due to raven attacks and wind.

A McKinley menu is subject to the conflicting demands imposed by climbing in cold weather, the need to maximize calories while minimizing weight and the problem of acclimatization. Pure fat contains about 250 food calories per ounce. Pure carbohydrate contains about 112. Cold weather and hard work demand lots of calories, and heavy packs are a drag, so fatty foods with lots of calories per ounce are a natural choice. Unfortunately, fats require more oxygen to digest than carbohydrates. According to Dr. Charles S. Houston, writing in the 1979 American Alpine Journal, clear proof exists that an almost pure carbohydrate diet increases a person's effective altitude tolerance by 2,000 feet. According to Dr. Peter Hackett, one of the nation's leading authorities on mountain sickness, a diet of 70 to 80 percent carbohydrates during the first few days at a higher elevation increases blood oxygen levels and helps reduce the symptoms of mountain sickness. Hackett adds, however, that the loss of appetite with altitude, which leads to an inadequate food intake, is probably the root cause of deterioration up high. The total number of calories, therefore, becomes more important than the ratio of fats to carbohydrates. The major problem, according to Hackett, is getting people to eat enough. Cold weather and strenuous activity mean climbers on McKinley need from 4,500 to 6,000 calories per person per day.

Recommended Diet

For one person for one day:

cold or hot cereal	4-6 ozs.
powdered milk	1-2 ozs.
cocoa	2-3 ozs.
margarine	1.3 ozs. (third of stick)
hard or cream cheese	3-4 ozs.
logan bread	4 ozs. (one thick slice)
chocolate	2-3 ozs.
gorp	4-5 ozs.
bagel	2 ozs.
instant soup	1-2 oz.
freeze-dried dinner	4 ozs.
two tea bags	0.2 ozs.
instant coffee	0.1 ozs.
NutraSweet Kool-Aid	0.1 ozs
total	**28.7 – 36.7 ozs.**

Protein is essential for the body to build cell walls, muscles, hormones and enzymes. Eating a pure carbohydrate diet for the entire expedition would probably be unwise. Estimates of protein requirements vary from 2 to 4 ounces per day for a 155-pound man, or about 1 gram per kilogram of body weight.

The best diet for McKinley is probably a compromise mixing fats, protein and carbohydrates. Much of McKinley lies below the elevation at which altitude has a major effect on the body. The diet outlined in the sidebar seems to work well for most people.

Hot cereal is one of the first foods that many people reject on a long trip. I remember cooking up gallons of oatmeal and cream of wheat for a 13-man expedition I guided in July, 1982, then throwing three-quarters of it into the latrine bag. Cold cereal can be made hot, if desired. On that trip, we also brought lots of summer sausage and hard salami. On the first day, everyone considered it a treat and ate their fill. That afternoon, however, their stomachs rebelled as we hauled loads in the intense heat of a sunny, windless day on the lower Kahiltna. The rest of the sausage went uneaten. Sweet foods like chocolate and candy bars are easy to carry, keep well and seem like they should be palatable under any circumstances. After all, most people try to restrict their intake of sweet junk food while they're at home. An expedition seems like a wonderful excuse to pig out on forbidden fruit. In truth, people often get tired of a diet that relies too heavily on sweets. One client in 1982 told me after a week on the mountain that he never wanted to see another Milky Way bar as long as he lived.

One to two ounces of powdered milk per day is plenty for cereal, tea and coffee. There's usually some left over to stretch and enrich hot cocoa and soup. Milk is also a good drink on its own.

Two to three ounces of cocoa is enough for two big cups per person per day. Hot spiced apple cider and hot eggnog are excellent substitutes.

The quantity of margarine suggested is one-third of a stick, convenient if you're packing three days of food for one person in one bag. Other ways of packing may make 1 or 2 ounces of margarine per person per day more convenient.

Both cream cheese and hard cheese are rich in fat, always craved in the cold. They taste good by themselves or melted into a freeze-dried dinner.

Logan bread is a dense, mildly sweet homemade bread rich with eggs, honey, walnuts and dates. The recipe, outlined in the sidebar, is simple. Fig bars and other dense, soft, hard-to-crush cookies can be substituted for the logan bread.

M&Ms are a good form of chocolate because they don't crush. Other forms of solid chocolate are also good. Nougat-filled candy bars get smashed and gush all over their bags.

Any combination of nuts, dried fruit, sunflower seeds, coconut, chocolate or carob bits and soy nuts makes a good gorp ("Good Old Raisins and Peanuts"). Consider bringing several different kinds to provide variety.

Bagels are quite palatable everywhere on the climb. They keep well, are easily thawed (stick them in your armpit, inside a plastic bag), taste good and sit easy in the stomach. Crackers are a good substitute, but they're bulky and tend to degenerate into croutons within a few days.

Instant soups, such as Lipton Cup-O-Soup, provide a good beginning to a meal. Each one-ounce packet serves one person. No cooking is required. Everyone mixes the soup in their own cup.

Logan Bread

3   cups flour (any mixture of whole wheat and rye)
¾   cup wheat germ
¼   cup brown sugar
½   cup powdered milk
1   cup oil
½   cup honey
¼   cup molasses
¼   cup sorghum syrup or maple syrup (any combination of these four sweeteners totaling one cup works fine)
½   cup shelled walnuts or pecans
1   cup dried fruit (raisins, dates, apricots, peaches, etc.)
6   eggs

Beat all the ingredients together in a large bowl. Pat down into two greased 5x9 loaf pans. Bake at 275 degrees F for two hours or until a toothpick comes out clean. The bread is very heavy and dense. Each loaf weighs 24 ounces.

Freeze-dried dinners that require no cooking, just soaking in boiling water, are extremely convenient. They require a minimum amount of fuel, leave the pot clean and get supper into hungry bellies as fast as possible. A dollop of butter and a chunk of cheese add a lot of appeal. Some of the blander meals benefit from a dash of garlic powder, curry or other spices. Climbers flying in from abroad (except Canadians) should note that U.S. Customs will not allow them to bring in freeze-dried food containing meat.

Climbers with time and inclination can create cheaper and sometimes tastier equivalents to freeze-dried food by combining instant rice, instant potatoes or pasta with instant soups and freeze-dried vegetables. Supermarkets stock a variety of quick-cooking pasta and rice dishes that can be quite palatable. Canned fish and meat add flavor and the feeling of eating real food but also add a lot of weight. It's a good idea to experiment with recipes beforehand, not only to test for flavor, but also to determine the filling power of a particular quantity of raw ingredients. One possible compromise: Use foods that require cooking and weigh more down low, with freeze-dried meals reserved for up high.

Bear in mind that everything you eat (except dishes right off the stove) is likely to be frozen as hard as granite. Butter and peanut butter, for example, practically become brittle at temperatures around zero. Spreading them on a bagel or cracker is nearly impossible. Margarine gets very firm in the cold, but doesn't freeze as hard as butter. Cereal, gorp, logan bread and most candy bars and granola bars are palatable when frozen. Hard cheese and cream cheese are best thawed by chunking them up into a hot freeze-dried dinner.

Melted snow tastes pretty plain after awhile, and people tend to drink less than their bodies need. Flavored drink mixes encourage people to stay hydrated. I prefer the artificially sweetened drink mixes, made half-strength, because they give water some flavor without promoting the flash and crash, hyperglycemic/hypoglycemic cycle that sugar-sweetened drinks can create. The drink mixes also weigh next to nothing. Some people bring various electrolyte replacement drinks.

On most of my expeditions, I've organized the food into "three-day bags," each containing food for one person for three days. The bag's contents vary in the type of cereal, gorp, cheese and freeze-dried dinners they contain, but the total weight is always the same. Every three days, each team member grabs a new three-day bag out of the pile, which he eats from for the next three days. Team members can keep any extra food if they feel they might want it later, or donate it to the extra food bag, where it becomes fair game for anyone with the munchies. Organization by three-day units creates bags of a size that stow easily in a pack. Climbers can vary their diet by eating their cereal for lunch and their gorp for breakfast, if they want. On alpine-style climbs, each climber carries all his own food, so each person's pack diminishes in weight at the same rate. The system saves packaging because you can put three days worth of cereal, powdered milk, cocoa, gorp, etc., into one small bag. It's also easy to leave behind a set number of days, for example, in a food cache at base camp. My preferences may be colored by my experiences on alpine-style climbs where food was chronically short, but it seems to me that an indisputably clear-cut method of dividing the food, (such as each person carrying his own) eliminates any possibility of disputes. One drawback of this system is that it assumes that every dinner will be freeze-dried and packed in individual portions.

One logical and popular alternative to packing in three-day bags is to pack all the food for the entire team for one day into one bag. The bags can be numbered for each day of the trip, with the lower-numbered bags containing the heavier, low-altitude rations if you have different menus for different parts of the trip. If you pack in one-day bags, you need to determine some simple, equitable method of dividing up the meals each day. For example, on McKinley people nibble constantly during the day, rather than sitting down for one big group meal at midday. It's usually most convenient, therefore, if each person carries his own lunch.

In addition to the edibles, each food bag should contain a book of matches inside a plastic bag. Each team member also should carry two lighters, with a few spares tucked away deep in the bottom of your repair kit. When wet or cold, cigarette lighters work poorly. Lighters are another item you should keep in an inside pocket.

Each climber should carry a large plastic cup (a two-cup measuring cup is convenient), a spoon and possibly a fork, depending on the menu. Carrying a large bowl as well makes it possible to drink something hot and eat at the same time instead of sequentially. Plastic cups and bowls can get brittle in the cold, so pack them away carefully.

One 1½ quart pot is the minimum for a team of two. Larger teams require more and larger pots. Those planning to cook food in the pot (instead of simply boiling water in it) should also bring a scouring pad for clean-up.

Most foods, as they come from the supermarket, are swaddled in far too much packaging. Climbers can save an amazing amount of bulk and weight by carrying, for example, a small plastic bag containing six ounces of cocoa rather than six individual one-ounce packets. The same is true of the popular Lipton soup mixes that make individual one-cup servings. Repacking food also reduces the amount of trash which must be carried off the mountain. Large empty food bags can be reused as trash bags. If your style of food packing doesn't generate large empty bags, bring along a couple to serve as trash bags. All powdered foods (milk, cocoa, soup) should be double-bagged. The margarine stick deserves a bag of its own. The other foods can be grouped as convenient.

On McKinley, all drinking and cooking water is obtained by melting snow. A few cases have been reported where climbers developed gastrointestinal diseases, probably by drinking fecal-contaminated melted snow. Some climbers have responded by purifying their melted snow by boiling, filtering or adding iodine. So far, however, problems with contaminated snow seem rare. If you're careful to select clean snow for melting, there should be no need to purify it. Freshly fallen snow should always be safe. Snow dug up well away from camp is more likely to be pure than snow near camp. The few cases of gastrointestinal disease that have occurred should reinforce for everyone the need to practice the sanitation procedures discussed in the chapter on Environmental Considerations.

Most West Buttress expeditions start up the mountain with 17 to 25 days of food. The Muldrow route requires more, from 21 to 35 days. Climbers going alpine-style usually start the actual climbing on the Cassin and West Rib with eight to 12 days. Another few days should be allotted for the glacier approach. Better yet, allow a week for the approach and go up to 14,300 feet on the West Buttress to acclimatize before starting the technical portion of the route. The South Buttress from the east fork of the Kahiltna could easily take as long as the West Buttress if the team is ferrying loads: 17 to 25 days. All climbers should leave a well-marked cache of six days of food and fuel at their fly-out point to ensure they won't starve if the glacier pilot is delayed by bad weather.

Leaving camp at 7,000 feet on Kahiltna Glacier.
Photo: Glenn Randall

The Problems of High Altitude

McKINLEY'S ALTITUDE AND FAR NORTHERN LATITUDE can cause problems that mountaineers who've climbed only in the Lower 48 during the summer have probably never had to face. Most common is acute mountain sickness, a malady that can be mild or severe. Mountaineers who ignore the early symptoms of AMS can develop two life-threatening illnesses: pulmonary edema and cerebral edema. Like AMS, both diseases are an outgrowth of the body's failure to adapt to the lower atmospheric pressure found at high altitude. All McKinley climbers, whether properly acclimatized or not, are susceptible to two additional problems: hypothermia and frostbite. The three are often intermixed, however, with one reinforcing the other. Knowledge, adequate equipment, an appropriate rate of ascent and diligent body maintenance on the mountain are the keys to a healthy expedition.

Acute Mountain Sickness

Serious mountain sickness can strike far lower than most climbers think. Two Japanese climbers developed high-altitude cerebral edema, the accumulation of fluid in the brain, well below 13,000 feet on the West Buttress. Both died. In one case, carbon monoxide fumes from cooking in a closed tent may have contributed to the problem. Details in the other case are unknown. A climber who had worked at a ski area at 9,000 feet all winter developed high-altitude pulmonary edema, the accumulation of fluid in the lungs, at 10,000 feet on the West Buttress. His companions evacuated him on a sled since he could no longer walk. A hiker in California's Sierra Nevada developed high-altitude pulmonary edema at 8,000 feet. He spent five days in a hospital on oxygen before recovering. Everyone venturing onto McKinley should know how to prevent, recognize and treat acute mountain sickness and its corollaries, pulmonary and cerebral edema.

High altitude illnesses are caused by a decreased concentration of oxygen in the blood, although the exact mechanism is still unclear. The body's failure to adjust to the lower supply of oxygen at altitude is the root cause of mountain sickness.

Adaptation to high altitude involves many changes. The depth and rate of breathing increase. Pressure in the pulmonary arteries goes up, forcing more blood through the capillaries in the lungs. That, in turn, increases the lung's capacity to absorb oxygen. The output of the heart increases for the first few days at a higher elevation, sending more oxygenated blood to the tissues. The bone marrow increases its production of red blood cells, which means that the blood can carry more oxygen. Changes in the chemistry of the blood allow the red blood cells to release their oxygen more easily.

The respiratory and biochemical changes require six to eight days. The red blood cell count reaches 90 percent of maximum in about six weeks. Overall, about 80 percent of the adaptation is complete in 10 days. Ninety-five percent is accomplished in six weeks. Further time at altitude increases performance very little.

Mountain sickness begins when people climb too high too fast. How fast is too fast varies from individual to individual and from time to time for the same individual. In 1982, I climbed McKinley twice in one season. During the first of those two climbs, Peter Metcalf and I ascended from the glacier at 8,000 feet to the summit at 20,320 feet in nine days. Peter had a severe headache during most of the summit day. I had a bad headache only briefly. One year later, Peter and I climbed a new route on the north face of Mt. Foraker. I developed pulmonary edema at 15,000 feet, four days after leaving the glacier at 6,000 feet. Peter had severe headaches, but didn't get pulmonary edema. On McKinley, we had taken seven days to reach 15,000 feet — in retrospect, probably just barely enough.

The early stages of acute mountain sickness resemble a hangover. The first symptom is usually a headache. Don't be worried by a mild headache cured by a night's rest. Moderate or severe headaches that survive a night's sleep, or appear during sleep, and are not relieved with aspirin, are more serious. Other symptoms, if not already present, will usually appear if the climber goes higher without taking more time for acclimatization. If the headache persists through a second night, the climber should descend. Losing 1,000 to 1,500 feet usually will relieve the headache. Five minutes of gentle but firm massage of the artery just in front of the middle of the ear may help an altitude headache in ways not fully understood.

Climbers who have difficulty falling asleep and staying asleep, and who awaken feeling tired in the morning, should watch for more serious symptoms of acute mountain sickness. Mild appetite loss is another warning sign. Both symptoms generally improve during the second week at altitude. Another yellow flag is vomiting, which both weakens and dehydrates a person. Stomach flu could be the culprit, if no other altitude symptoms are present. Regardless of the cause, however, someone vomiting frequently should be taken to lower altitudes immediately, before he/she becomes too weak to walk. Compazine or Phenergan suppositories can help. Drugs given orally are usually lost in the next attack of vomiting.

A cough can be caused by breathing deeply in the cold, dry air, or by chest infection, or by incipient pulmonary edema, the accumulation of fluid in the lungs. A cough present only during exertion, which does not affect strength and is relieved by throat lozenges, drinking plenty of fluids and breathing steam, is most likely a dry-air cough, which is only a nuisance. A cough accompanied by reduced endurance, a feeling of fullness or heaviness in the chest and breathlessness either while working or at rest (compared to companions) is more likely to indicate early pulmonary edema. Chest infections are difficult to distinguish from pulmonary edema. However, infection predisposes a person to pulmonary edema, and both may be present. Descent is mandatory if either a chest infection or pulmonary edema is suspected. Pulmonary edema almost always improves with a descent of 3,000 feet or less. Many victims of pulmonary edema have found that if they descend 3,000 feet, recuperate, then regain altitude slowly, allowing plenty of time for acclimatization, they can continue to the summit safely.

Periodic breathing, also called Cheyne-Stokes respiration, is an alarming but not necessarily dangerous symptom of acute mountain sickness in which a person typically takes three or four breaths, then stops breathing for 10 or 15 seconds. Changes in the control of breathing within the brain cause the problem, which is common above 13,000 feet and may be seen as low as 8,000 feet. Unless accompanied by other symptoms, don't be alarmed by periodic breathing.

Lassitude, another altitude complaint, can resemble hypothermia or exhaustion. A person who scarcely has the energy to eat, drink or speak, who does not recover with food and a night's rest, and who becomes progressively worse over 24 to 48 hours, is suffering from severe lassitude; this is cause for immediate descent.

Loss of coordination, called ataxia, can mean lack of oxygen is affecting the cerebellum, which controls balance and spatial orientation. Everyone suspected of suffering from altitude illness should be tested for ataxia with these simple procedures. Sobriety is a prerequisite. The heel-to-toe walking test requires the subject to walk slowly along a straight line. At each step, the subject places the heel of one boot immediately in front of the toe of the other. Normal subjects can walk the line without difficulty. Mildly ataxic subjects sway noticeably, but can walk 10 or 12 feet without falling. Moderately ataxic subjects will probably step off the line or stagger. Severely ataxic people will fall down. For comparison, have a healthy person take the same test.

The Romberg test of coordination requires the subject to stand with feet together, arms at the sides. The tester encircles the subject at chest level with his arms without allowing his arms to touch the subject, then tells the subject to close his eyes. A healthy person can stand in balance. Ataxic subjects will sway within 10 or 15 seconds.

Altitude-ataxia must be distinguished from ataxia caused by hypothermia, and ataxia due to exhaustion, both of which respond to rest, food and warmth. Altitude-ataxia does not respond to these treatments. If altitude-ataxia is present, the person should descend 1,000 to 3,000 feet immediately. Untreated victims can lose the ability to walk in six to 12 hours.

French ski patrollers change oxygen bottles for a pulmonary edema victim at 11,000 feet on the West Buttress.
Photo: Glenn Randall

Reduced urine output is another danger sign, because it indicates either dehydration, a predisposing factor for mountain sickness, or retention of fluids, which is indicative of the onset of altitude illness itself.

Peripheral edema is the accumulation of excessive fluid in the hands, feet, ankles or face. Swollen hands are the most common and most likely to be caused by problems other than altitude, such as pack-strap compression, restrictive clothing, sun or cold. Swollen feet and ankles are rare. Approximately three-quarters of those with swollen faces not caused by sunburn will have other symptoms of mountain sickness that will determine treatment. Peripheral edema by itself is not cause for descent.

Retinal hemorrhage, (bleeding in the retina), while fairly common, can usually only be detected with an opthalmoscope. Occasionally, the hemorrhage will be large enough to cause a noticeable blind spot. In those cases, the climber should descend. These hemorrhages heal spontaneously upon return to lower altitudes and cause no long-term damage.

All of these symptoms of altitude sickness can be present in varying degrees. A mild headache, some shortness of breath, loss of appetite and restless sleep means a person should slow the rate of ascent, and perhaps take another day or night to acclimatize. If these symptoms worsen to the point that the victim is quite uncomfortable, however, further acclimatization is essential. Climbers with severe symptoms should not go higher! If the symptoms worsen further, descent is by far the best treatment - the sooner and farther the better. Continued ascent, or even remaining at the same altitude, can mean the development of life-threatening cerebral or pulmonary edema.

Cerebral edema, the swelling of the brain through the accumulation of fluid, causes severe headache, vomiting, ataxia, lassitude and reduced urine output. It usually develops over several days. A day or two of mild symptoms, followed by a day or two of quite uncomfortable symptoms, can be followed in as little as 12 hours by unconsciousness. Victims sometimes become completely disoriented or begin hallucinating. Immediate descent, even in the middle of the night, can save a life. Waiting for a rescue or a doctor is inexcusable.

The first signs of pulmonary edema, the accumulation of fluid in the lungs, are the pronounced breathlessness, reduced exercise capacity and cough described previously. An increased pulse and respiration rate are also common and can be detected by comparison with the rates of healthy people. Respiration rate after a 10-minute rest may be 26 breaths per minute or higher. The other symptoms of mountain sickness are usually present as well.

As the amount of fluid in the lungs increases, the lips and fingernails turn blue. Comparison with the lips and nails of a healthy person should be done in daylight, outside a tent. The victim also coughs up pinkish or rusty-colored fluid. Descent should not be delayed! Early detection of pulmonary edema and rapid descent mean quicker recovery with less altitude loss.

Many drugs have been used in the prevention and treatment of mountain sickness, but none can guarantee either complete immunity or a cure. The best preventative is to go high slowly. Above 10,000 feet, move camp upward no more than 1,000 feet per day. The sleeping altitude is critical, not the amount of elevation gained and lost. Sleep an extra night at the same altitude after every 3,000 feet of gain above 10,000 feet. Concentrating on deep breathing exercises and increasing the ratio of breaths to steps can also be helpful. Drink enough to keep your urine clear, even if that means chugging four or five quarts a day. Alcohol may be harmful because of its diuretic action. Sherpa wisdom dictates never getting drunk the first night at altitude. Avoid exhaustion and eat a diet high in carbohydrates. You should also avoid excessive salt, which can cause fluid retention and thus a predisposition to edema. Still, some people get sick even though they take all the recommended precautions.

Climbers intent on an alpine-style ascent of McKinley must find a delicate balance between climbing the mountain quickly enough to avoid exhausting their limited food supplies and climbing slowly enough to avoid contracting pulmonary or cerebral edema. Ten or twelve days of food is about all you can carry on an alpine-style ascent, yet few people acclimatize quickly enough to climb safely to McKinley's summit in such a short time. On the West Buttress, most climbers who avoid becoming sick take five to seven days to reach 14,300 feet. Adopting the same prudent pace on an alpine-style climb would leave climbers 6,000 vertical feet below the summit with at most a week's worth of food, and possibly as little as three days – clearly a very thin margin, given the need to acclimatize and the possibility of lengthy storms. Most climbers attempting alpine-style ascents choose to risk altitude sickness rather than risk running out of food. They climb as fast as they can when the weather is good, figuring they'll hole up if the weather goes sour and acclimatize then. Many climbers have developed acute mountain sickness as a result, some seriously.

There is a way to make the balancing act between food supply and acclimatization tip steeply in your favor. Climbers who want to try a route on McKinley's south or west face, such as the West Rib or Cassin, should seriously consider taking a week to climb to 14,300 feet on the West Buttress first, then spend several nights there to acclimatize before beginning their route. This highly recommended tactic will increase both the safety of your climb and your enjoyment of it. Who wants to reach the summit gasping, nauseated and with a headache that feels like a Norse god has buried his battle-ax in your skull? Most climbers doing a south-face route descend via the West Buttress. If that's your plan, consider caching a couple of days of food and fuel at 17,200 feet on the West Buttress, which will reduce your load on the actual climb and help you feel productive as you acclimatize at 14,300 feet. Just be sure you pick up your cache on the way down.

McKinley expeditions should carry a few drugs. Aspirin can alleviate the mild headaches that afflict nearly everyone at altitude at one time or another. A cup of caffeinated coffee or tea can also be helpful. Acetazolamide (Diamox) does aid acclimatization for most people, though it is a potent drug and cannot be considered a guarantee against getting sick. Diamox increases the acidity of the blood, allowing a person to hyperventilate more without experiencing ill effects; it also acts as a breathing stimulant during sleep at high altitude.

On the negative side, Diamox increases urine output, potentially causing dehydration unless the climber is careful to replace the fluids. It also can cause numbness and tingling in the fingers, toes and face. Some people find it causes nausea and drowsiness and makes beer taste strange. Diamox is a member of the group of anti-bacterial medications called sulfa drugs. People who are sensitive to sulfa drugs should not take Diamox, which could cause an allergic reaction. Symptoms of a reaction could include rashes, nausea, wheezing, or, rarely, life-threatening shock.

Diamox is recommended as a preventative for someone who must go high fast and stay high, such as a rescuer, or for someone who routinely suffers from mountain sickness despite following the procedures suggested above. It can also be used to treat mild mountain sickness. The recommended dosage for a man of average weight (160 lbs.) is 250 mg twice a day. Women of average weight, smaller men and adolescents should take 125 mg twice a day. Climbers using the drug for prevention should begin taking it 24 hours prior to going to altitude, and continue it for the first day or two after reaching altitude. If symptoms of mountain sickness occur, treatment with the drug should resume. If the drug is used solely for treatment, the patient should start taking it when the symptoms appear and continue taking it for 24 to 48 hours, or until the symptoms disappear.

Dr. Peter Hackett, an authority on mountain sickness, recommends dexamethasone (Decadron) as a treatment for moderate to severe altitude illness, particularly cases involving cerebral symptoms such as ataxia. It has not been shown to be effective against high-altitude pulmonary edema. As a general rule, it should not be used as a preventative except, possibly, by people with a strong susceptibility to acute mountain sickness, particularly those who are allergic to Diamox. Some recent studies have shown that Decadron can be effective in treating the symptoms of high-altitude cerebral edema. According to Dr. Hackett, the drug should definitely be given to climbers at altitude who develop loss of coordination (ataxia). Climbers who become confused or disoriented, who are hallucinating or unresponsive, should be given Decadron, then taken to a lower altitude immediately. Unlike Diamox, Decadron does not aid the body's process of acclimatization. If discontinued too soon, before the body has had a chance to acclimatize, illness can result. The recommended dosage is 4 mg every six hours. It should be continued until the victim reaches a lower altitude or until all symptoms have disappeared. If treatment lasts more than 24 hours, the dosage should gradually be reduced to 2 mg every six hours (four doses per day). If symptoms of mountain sickness recur, a full dosage of 4 mg every six hours should be resumed until the victim can be brought to a lower altitude. Slow acclimatization is still the best preventative; rapid descent is still the only sure cure. For a more complete discussion of drugs at altitude, see Dr. Hackett's chapter in *Surviving Denali* (Jonathan Waterman, American Alpine Club Press, 1991).

Susceptibility to mountain sickness varies widely among individuals. At present, no sea-level predictors of susceptibility exist. Dr. Hackett theorizes that a correlation exists between blood oxygenation levels under various conditions and susceptibility to mountain sickness. In some people, blood oxygen levels drop during exercise. In others, (probably mostly the same individuals), blood oxygen levels drop during exposure to high altitude. People with a "low hypoxic drive to breathe" simply don't breathe hard enough and deep enough to maintain their blood oxygen level at altitude. Dr. Hackett theorizes that those whose blood oxygen levels drop during exercise and those with a low hypoxic drive to breathe are those most susceptible to mountain sickness.

Good performance at altitude comes from physical fitness and the ability to acclimatize. Fitness comes from training; the hypoxic drive to breathe, and hence, probably, the ability to acclimatize, are hereditary. Fitness and the ability to acclimatize are completely unrelated. In fact, some world-class athletes do not acclimatize well. They have a low hypoxic drive to breathe, which aids in preventing breathlessness during exercise at sea-level, but reduces their ability to acclimatize.

Complete adaptation to altitude takes too long to be a reasonable goal for mountaineers. The body of a person living at 14,000 feet, for example, will continue adapting for two and a half years. However, forty-eight hours without symptoms at a given altitude, assuming early pulmonary edema can be recognized, is assurance that no serious illness will strike and that more altitude can be safely gained. Loss of acclimatization is rapid. A well-acclimated person who descends to sea-level for two days, then re-ascends, is susceptible.

To learn more about high-altitude disease, I highly recommend Dr. Hackett's book, *Mountain Sickness: Prevention, Recognition and Treatment* (American Alpine Club, 1980). I am indebted to him for his thoughtful review of the information presented here.

Hypothermia

Hypothermia – subnormal body temperature – can attack with astonishing speed. I learned that the hard way when I took a team of eight clients from 14,300 feet to 17,200 feet on the West Buttress in July, 1982. Among my clients was a nurse named Marilyn whose enormous drive seemed adequate compensation for her lack of fitness. When we arrived at 17,200 feet, however, a frosty wind began blowing. We started digging a snow cave – a cold, hard, wet job under the best of circumstances. Marilyn seemed to be holding up well, but when we erected a tent as a temporary shelter so people could add clothing in comfort, Marilyn was among the first to slip inside. Soon, another client emerged from the tent after donning another sweater.

"You'd better check on Marilyn," he said. "She seems to be getting a bit hypothermic."

Not five minutes had elapsed since I'd last seen her. I crawled into the tent. Although she was cocooned in her sleeping bag, she was shaking uncontrollably. I called her name. She did not respond. Immediately, I began stripping off some of her outer clothing while a client located two sleeping bags that could be zipped together. Then, an assistant and I shed our outer clothing

Gordy Vernon and Marilyn Allen near the summit of McKinley.
Photo: Glenn Randall

and crawled in with Marilyn. We wanted no insulating clothing to prevent our body heat from reaching her. Outside, another client lighted a stove. Marilyn was far too comatose to drink or eat, but I wanted the additional warmth of hot water bottles for her as soon as possible. Later, when she was alert, she could have a hot, sweet drink. I guessed that her weak stomach had prevented her from eating all day.

In perhaps half an hour, she came out of her delirium and could sip a little fruit drink. In a few hours, she seemed completely recovered. Still, she had been far too close to the edge for comfort. A combination of wind, cold, evaporation of sweat after hard exercise, altitude and lack of food and water had created a real emergency. Four days later, however, to my astonishment, she reached the summit.

The body's temperature control mechanism is surprisingly unstable. According to Dr. William Mills, an Anchorage physician who is one of the nation's foremost authorities on cold injury, a drop in core temperature of only 4½ degrees F puts the mechanism in jeopardy. If cooling persists, the body may lose the ability to rewarm itself, regardless of how much insulation is added. Unless rescuers can actively warm the victim, death is assured.

The body responds first to cold by shivering and withdrawing blood from the extremities to preserve heat in the core. As cooling continues, the signs of hypothermia appear: numb, useless hands, frequent stumbling, slurred speech, slow, shallow breathing, gray or bluish skin, lethargy, confusion and forgetfulness. Shivering may or may not continue. At a core temperature of about 90 degrees F, most victims slip into a coma. Heart failure and death can occur before the core temperature reaches 88 degrees, though some victims have been revived after their core temperature has plunged much lower.

Treatment is simple: rewarming, starting with the trunk and head. Warm clothing provides only insulation. Even perfect insulation only allows the body to heat the surrounding air to its own depressed temperature. External heat must be applied. The easiest, most effective method is to zip two sleeping bags together, put the victim inside, then have a warm rescuer crawl in as well. Remove some of both the victim's and the rescuer's outer clothing so the rescuer's body heat can reach the victim more easily. Water bottles filled with hot water also help. Giving a victim alcohol is a bad idea. Alcohol stimulates circulation in the extremities. That may make the victim feel better, but it leads to further core cooling.

Hot drinks are a good way to help warm a conscious victim. They also combat the dehydration commonly found in hypothermia victims. As the body shuts down blood flow to the extremities, the blood volume in the core goes up. The kidneys respond by extracting the apparently excess water from the blood and sending it to the bladder for elimination, a phenomenon called "cold diuresis." When the victim is warmed, blood again flows in usual quantities to the limbs. Blood volume in the core drops below normal. Hot liquids help correct the problem.

The first key to staying warm is staying dry. Sweating heavily can be almost as bad as getting soaked by melting snow. Regardless of the source of the moisture, evaporation will chill you once you stop moving. Frequent snacking helps maintain the body's ability to generate heat. Going hungry can lead to increased acidity of the blood, which aggravates both fatigue and hypothermia. Munching tidbits, even if the volume is inadequate to entirely restore the body's energy level, can help prevent this increased acidity. Even a well-fed climber, if very tired, is more susceptible to hypothermia than a rested one.

Dehydration can be a contributing factor in hypothermia as well as a result. Inadequate fluid intake has other bad effects as well. Besides pre-disposing a climber to altitude sickness, dehydration's symptoms can include weakness, fatigue, dizziness and a tendency to faint upon standing; a tendency to develop severe shock following even minor injuries; and a tendency to form blood clots, which creates a danger that a clot will form somewhere in the body, break loose and lodge in the lungs. Altitude dulls the sensation of thirst, which means climbers must consciously force themselves to drink more than they think they want. You know you're drinking enough if your urine is gin clear.

Frostbite

The constriction of blood vessels in the hands and feet caused by dehydration and hypothermia frequently exacerbates another cold injury: frostbite. The freezing of tissue also can occur simply through brief exposure of bare skin to cold, particularly if the skin touches cold metal. Spilling sub-zero white gas on bare skin, or unscrewing a butane fuel cartridge before it's quite empty and letting some of the butane reach your bare hand, can cause instant frostbite. Frozen tissue is particularly susceptible to damage during thawing, which makes the means of thawing crucial.

For almost a century and a half, nearly all doctors used the treatment prescribed by Baron Larrey, surgeon-in-charge of Napoleon's Grand Army during the retreat from Moscow in the winter of 1812-13. Larrey saw men with frozen hands and feet thaw them before a roaring bivouac fire, then noted the hideous gangrene that followed. From this he concluded that heat should be avoided in the treatment of frostbite, and that friction massage with ice or snow was the treatment of choice. Some out-of-date survival manuals still give the same bad advice.

Larrey's observations were correct in one respect. Thawing with excessive heat, such as over a stove or in hot water, is the worst possible treatment. Next in line, however, comes friction massage with snow. Both usually result in large losses of flesh. Gradual thawing at room temperature, inside a sleeping bag for example, also is unsatisfactory, especially in severe cases, because the degree of damage is directly related to the length of time the part remains frozen.

The best treatment is rapid rewarming in a water bath at 90 to 110 degrees, according to Dr. Mills of Anchorage. In no case should the temperature of the bath exceed 115 degrees. Admittedly, it may be rather hard to use this method if the part you're trying to thaw is your nose. Use the palm of your bare hand, unless your first name is Cyrano. The thawing part should never be rubbed, as the skin and underlying tissue will be quite fragile. The victim should avoid tobacco. Nicotine hinders the already damaged circulation. Thawing is often painful. Keep strong pain killers handy.

Thawing should continue until the afflicted part flushes pink clear to the tip, is warm to the touch and remains flushed when removed from the bath. Don't worry about a temporary purplish color. If the purple color persists, however, it may mean that swelling caused by a bone fracture, sprain or soft tissue injury is obstructing the return of blood to the heart. Get off the mountain and see a doctor as soon as possible.

Some of Larrey's errors in developing a treatment for frostbite came from his failure to observe the progress of the same soldier over time. Often the thawed part would be refrozen the next day. This refreezing was as much to blame for the gangrene Larrey observed as the excessive heat used in thawing. Allowing a thawed part to refreeze is much worse than keeping it frozen for several hours – or even days – until it can be thawed permanently. Don't thaw a frostbitten finger or toe unless both the injured part and the patient can be kept warm throughout the descent. Frostbitten limbs on a patient who becomes chilled are highly susceptible to refreezing.

Large blisters usually appear within a few hours of thawing a severely frozen digit. Keep these blisters from rupturing. Their contents, and the flesh beneath, are usually sterile. Infection poses a serious danger to frostbite victims. Breaking the blisters will allow bacteria to enter the wound. Infection is particularly tough to battle in frostbite cases because the blood vessels in the frozen area usually are too damaged to conduct antibiotics to the infection. Keep frostbitten areas clean and protected from pressure and abrasion. Then get to a doctor.

Prevention of both frostbite and hypothermia requires, first, adequate equipment. Boots or gloves that constrict circulation are deadly. Equally important, however, is complete body maintenance. Unless you take care of your body's needs, the best equipment in the world will not prevent hypothermia and frostbite. It's critical to drink plenty of fluids, enough to keep your urine clear. Dehydration predisposes climbers to both frostbite and hypothermia. Nibble frequently even if you don't feel hungry. Be sure to remove your boots every night and replace your damp socks with dry ones. Dry the damp ones in your sleeping bag between yourself and several layers of clothing. Abstain from tobacco. Nicotine is a vasoconstrictor, which can predispose you to frostbite. If your toes or fingers do become numb, stop to warm them. If you're unsure whether your toes are getting frostbitten, stop, remove your boots and visually inspect them. If they're pale and numb, rewarm them by placing your bare feet on a companion's bare stomach. It's common for people's feet to get cold during the last-minute preparations before leaving high camp for the summit. If they don't rewarm within an hour or two after you begin climbing, however, frostbite is likely. There is no treatment that can repair the damage caused by frostbite; all doctors can do is minimize the damage by using proper thawing techniques and preventing complications. The absence of a cure makes prevention even more critical.

Other Health Problems

With our worship of the tanned, athletic look often comes a cavalier disregard for protecting our skin from the sun. On McKinley, the result is usually a stunning sunburn, not a stunning tan. Direct sunlight provides only a fraction of the burning rays. Reflection from snow-covered valley walls can cause severe burns. Snow reflects about 75 percent of the light striking it. Even in the shade, the sunlight scattered by the atmosphere, particularly on a day with a thin overcast, can cause burning. People who have never climbed at high altitude before often grossly underestimate the savage power of the sun on McKinley. By the time they recognize that using sunscreen twice a day is inadequate, it's too late – their skin is already peeling in patches the size of half-dollars. Apply the strongest sunblock you can find at least four times a day. I like sunscreens that rub in, leaving an invisible film on your skin. Apply the first layer of sunscreen each morning before you leave the tent, to allow the sunscreen to soak in before you expose your skin to the sun. An alternative is sunscreens containing zinc oxide or titanium dioxide. These rely on a thick, visible layer of the ointment to prevent rays from reaching the skin. They tend to sweat off easily, and smear over everything whenever the climber wipes his nose. An exception is the face paint clowns use, called clown white, which stays put and provides excellent protection, although the climber definitely looks like a refugee from Ringling Brothers. As mentioned in the personal equipment chapter, a nose guard can save a lot of grief.

Lips and the underside of the nose usually catch it the worst, so protect them well. Constant attention to applying sunscreens during the day and soothing lotions at night is required simply to battle sun and wind to a stalemate. Sunscreens and lip ointment should be kept warm and handy in an inside pocket. I apply lip ointment every hour or so.

Snowblindness is sunburn of the surface of the eye. No pain is felt while the damage is occurring. The first symptoms usually appear eight to 12 hours later. The

> ### First Aid
>
> A basic first aid kit for McKinley should include:
>
> Aspirin or acetominophen (Tylenol or the equivalent)
>
> Strong pain killer (consult the prescribing physician)
>
> Moleskin
>
> Large Band-Aid-type bandages
>
> Sterile gauze pads – four inch square
>
> Carlisle dressing (thick absorbent dressing for lacerations)
>
> Adhesive tape, two inches wide
>
> Elastic bandage
>
> Triangular bandage
>
> Roller gauze
>
> Antifungal foot powder or strong antiperspirant (for feet)
>
> Paper and pencil (to record symptoms and treatment so physician will know later what you did)
>
> Manual of medical care

initial feeling of dryness quickly becomes the feeling that the neighborhood bully just threw sand in your eyes. Blinking, movement, even light are painful. Cold compresses and staying somewhere dark may give some relief. Hourly application of an eye ointment or drops containing cortisone helps reduce inflammation, relieve pain and speed healing. The treatment should begin as soon as the first symptoms are noticed. Even without intervention, the eyes will heal themselves in a few days.

Prevention of snowblindness requires consistent use of sunglasses or goggles that block ultraviolet radiation. Sunglasses and goggles should permit passage of 10 percent or less of the ultraviolet wavelengths. Drugstore sunglasses are suspect. Sunglasses specifically designed for mountaineering, with side shields, are recommended.

Cold sores are a common problem. Regular use of a sunblock on your lips helps prevent them. Acidophilus or lysine pills may also help keep them away. Lip balms like Carmex or Herpecin-L are soothing if cold sores do occur.

Nasal decongestants such as Afrin can be helpful in relieving a high-altitude stuffy nose, which in turn causes people to breathe through their mouths while asleep, which then irritates the throat. Sleeping pills should be avoided because they can depress the respiratory system, causing or worsening high-altitude illness.

For a lecture on the perils, prevention and treatment of carbon monoxide poisoning caused by cooking in an unventilated tent or snow shelter, refer back to the section on stoves in the Group Gear chapter.

Miscellaneous

Other items to consider:

Phenergan or Compazine suppositories (for nausea)

Afrin (nasal decongestant)

Eye ointment or drops containing cortisone (for snowblindness)

Adhesive foam (for padding boot pressure points)

Antacid (for sour stomach)

Antihistamine (for colds)

Tweezers

Razor

Safety pins

Bandage scissors (with rounded tip)

Lomotil (for diarrhea)

Throat lozenges (for dry-air cough)

Thermometer reading down to 70 degrees F (for hypothermia victims)

See the text and consult a physician for recommendations on other drugs.

This chapter is not a complete discussion of the medical problems that may be encountered on McKinley. That subject is worth a book in itself. An excellent one is *Medicine for Mountaineering* (The Mountaineers, 1986). Every McKinley climber should study that book or its equivalent, then take an advanced first-aid class to get some hands-on experience.

Rescue

Most expeditions on McKinley carry a radio. Five-watt CBs are most commonly used. These are line-of-sight radios weighing about 2 pounds. Climbers on the west, south and east sides of McKinley should use channel 19, which is monitored by the Kahiltna Base radio operator, the National Park Service, glacier pilots and some bush residents. Climbers on the north side of the range should use channel 7, which is monitored by Camp Denali near Wonder Lake. From many points low on the mountain, these radio signals can only reach a plane flying overhead.

The crystal in a CB radio begins to go off-frequency in severe cold. Some models are more affected than others, but as a general rule, performance begins to deteriorate at around 0 degrees F. Batteries are even more subject to cold than the radio itself. Inserting warm batteries into a cold radio quickly chills the batteries. For best results, both the radio and the batteries must be warm. If your radio will let you insert a second crystal, put in a backup crystal for the same channel you will be using on the mountain. Five-watt CB radios cost $100 to $300. They can usually be rented from your pilot.

Although carrying a radio has saved many lives, climbers who, consciously or unconsciously, plan to rely on a radio to call for a helicopter in an emergency are fools. In recent years, there has been a disturbing trend among climbers to scream for rescue at the first sign of trouble, even when the party's size and strength would make it easy for the group to evacuate a member on its own. This is an invitation to disaster. Climbers with severe high-altitude pulmonary or cerebral edema can die if descent is delayed even a few hours. Bad weather frequently prevents the use of helicopters or fixed-wing airplanes for rescues. Even on blue-sky days, clear-air turbulence can prevent aircraft from operating. Helicopters about to embark on a rescue have broken down on the landing strip in Talkeetna. Rescues are very expensive, and frequently put a large number of other people at risk because of your problem. As one pilot put it, "Landing a Chinook helicopter on McKinley is like driving a car into a garage at 40 miles an hour and trying to stop before you hit the back wall." Remember also that nearby teams of climbers may be too weak to help. It's a rare team that's strong enough to help another party significantly above 17,000 feet.

Both common sense and climbing ethics dictate that an expedition in the Alaska Range should be self-sufficient and fully capable of extracting itself from any mess in which it finds itself. Prompt self-evacuation should always be the tactic of first resort in an emergency. Ideally, the victim should be moved all the way to the point where the climbers were landed. Lower elevations both help keep the victim alive and make it easier for a helicopter or fixed-wing plane to land if that becomes necessary. The denser air at lower elevations gives any kind of aircraft more lift, and usually means lower wind speeds. Plan ahead for the possibility that someone will get hurt or sick. For example, many climbers on the West Buttress bring at least one sled to 14,300 feet, because it would make it much easier to evacuate an incapacitated teammate.

If your team cannot manage a situation on its own, try to enlist the help of climbers nearby. As an absolute last resort, call the National Park Service, a bush pilot or the Kahiltna Base radio operator for an air evacuation. Then, pray that a suitable aircraft is available, that some brave pilot can be found, and that McKinley's winds are kind.

Dale Atkins crosses a crevasse at 15,500 feet on the West Buttress.
Photo: Glenn Randall

Campcraft and Glacier Travel

MT. MCKINLEY'S GLACIERS ARE AMONG THE WORLD'S most spectacular. The Kahiltna Glacier, the mountain's longest, extends some 36 miles from Kahiltna Pass at 10,000 feet to the final moraine-covered snout at only 1,000 feet. In many places, the Kahiltna is two miles wide. The crevasses on any big Alaska Range glacier can be so deep that the bottom is lost in blackness. Some crevasses on the Muldrow are 100 feet wide and a mile long. Other crevasses lie hidden beneath a fragile skin of snow that will collapse under a climber's weight.

Most mountaineers from the lower 48, (excepting those who have climbed in the Northwest), find that Alaska's glaciers pose unique problems and require the use of unfamiliar techniques. Even experienced Northwest climbers are likely to find that Alaskan glaciers are more dangerous than those with which they're familiar. Most of the Alaska Range's snow falls in late summer and fall. The winter itself is very cold and relatively dry, so snow bridges over crevasses aren't strengthened by the massive winter snowfalls common in the Northwest. When spring reaches Alaska, long, warm days cause meltwater to flow into the dry, porous snowpack, rapidly weakening the snow bridges. Few climbers venture onto McKinley after mid-July because the snow bridges are so weak and storms have become more and more frequent.

Climbers on any McKinley route usually spend at least several days camping and traveling on a glacier before starting the technical climbing. Most climbers regard the glacier travel as the warm-up, and so do not treat McKinley's glaciers with the seriousness they deserve. Crevasse falls have killed at least seven climbers and possibly account for the disappearance of two others. Unroped falls, including one taken by an experienced European guide on skis, accounted for five of those deaths. A thorough knowledge of glacier camping, traveling and crevasse-rescue techniques is mandatory. Perhaps even more important is the self-discipline to employ these techniques with relentless diligence, even when you're tired, cold, hungry and ready for camp — or ready for an exhilarating ski through fresh powder without the hassle of a rope to inhibit the joy.

A handbook of this length cannot replace a full-length climbing manual. Andy Selter's excellent book, *Glacier Travel and Crevasse Rescue* (The Mountaineers, 1990) should be required reading for those not well-versed in the subject. Theoretical knowledge, of course, is not enough. Climbers intending to tackle McKinley should locate a place to practice all aspects of crevasse rescue. Finding a crevasse is not a prerequisite. A small cliff will give you practice in the basics, which should include ascending a fixed rope with prusiks or Jumars, and rigging Z-pulley hauling systems. Experience in setting bombproof snow anchors in varied snow conditions is also essential, as is practice catching falls with a boot-ax belay. Learning to travel safely on a glacier is different in one peculiar way from learning to climb. The simple act of climbing on technical terrain is enough, over time, to hone your skills. Spending years traveling on glaciers, on the other hand, won't prepare you in the slightest for the very difficult challenge of rescuing someone after a bad crevasse fall. The only solution is to practice rescue techniques in advance.

The first rule of glacier travel is to travel roped. It doesn't matter whether there are visible crevasses to worry about or not. In May, 1982, Peter Metcalf and I climbed Reality Ridge on the southeast side of McKinley, then casually descended the West Buttress unroped. A month later, I descended the West Buttress again after guiding a group, and was horrified to discover that yawning crevasses, completely hidden during the ascent, had opened up and now bisected the trail, forcing significant detours.

Avoid traveling on glaciers below 10,000 feet during the hottest part of the day. Not only are the snow bridges weak and more likely to collapse under a climber's weight, but climbers dressed lightly for hard work in the hot sun are much more susceptible to hypothermia if they do go into a crevasse. Even a well-executed rescue can take long enough for an unprepared victim to become severely hypothermic.

Climbers should avoid traveling roped together too closely. Team members traveling only 20 or 30 feet apart risk being yanked into the same crevasse if one of the climbers falls through a snow bridge. Two climbers traveling 20 feet apart on the Peters Glacier in 1981 were pulled into the same crevasse. One died. Fifty feet should be the minimum distance between climbers, which means no more than three climbers on a 150-foot rope.

Almost as dangerous as unroped travel is letting a large amount of slack accumulate in the rope. It's unsafe, for example, to allow a climber to leave a rest stop unbelayed. In 1976, an unbelayed climber started leading the second rope out of a rest stop on the east fork of the Kahiltna, following the tracks made by two other climbers who had left just a minute before. The leader of the second rope – the third person to walk over the totally hidden crevasse – went 70 feet into the hole, crushing two vertebrae and breaking his arm. In 1984, the eighth climber in a team of nine, all following in each other's footsteps, plunged into a crevasse while descending the Muldrow. Fortunately, the experienced team had the rope taut and the uninjured climber was hauled out easily. The lesson is clear: The passage of two, three, even half a dozen climbers over an area does not guarantee safety. Given the time-consuming difficulty of setting good snow anchors, climbers should consider remaining spread out, with the rope fairly taut between them, when taking a rest stop.

If someone does go in, everyone else on the rope should drop into self-arrest position instantly. With good rope management, the fallen climber is usually uninjured and not too deep in the crevasse. If the crevasse lip is not severely undercut, the climber sometimes can simply attach his ascenders or prusiks to the rope to which he's tied and make his escape. If, as is common, the rope has sawed into the lip of the crevasse, the climbers outside must pad the crevasse's lip with an ice ax or pack (anchored, of course), and throw the fallen climber another rope, or the opposite end of the rope to which the climber is tied. The fallen climber uses the second rope to ascend. The second rope can be anchored to a snow fluke, picket, ice screws, buried pack or buried skis. As in rock climbing, never trust just one anchor. Always back it up. In many cases, two pairs of anchors, with the tension equalized between the components of each pair, are required for real security. Anyone approaching the crevasse to pad the lip or talk to the fallen climber must be on a tight, solid belay. It's often helpful, and sometimes essential, for someone to help the fallen climber back over the overhanging lip of the crevasse. Don't assume that there is only one hidden crevasse in the vicinity.

A heavy pack makes the whole operation vastly more difficult. Without a chest harness, a heavy pack often leaves the fallen climber hanging upside down. To fully appreciate the severity of that predicament, suspend yourself upside down from a tree limb for a while and feel the blood begin to pound in your temples. If you do wear a chest harness, don't tie the rope to it – you could hang yourself from it in more ways than one. Instead, tie the rope to your sit harness as you normally would, then run the rope through a carabiner on your chest harness. With or without a chest harness, the first step a fallen climber with a heavy load usually must take is to shed his pack and hang it from the climbing rope with a prusik knot. It's a good idea to attach a sling to your pack before embarking on a glacier so that you can tie off your pack before actually removing it from your back.

Crevasse rescue (Z-pulley) system.
Drawing: Marj Leggitt

The worst kind of crevasse rescues are those in which the fallen climber is too injured to get out alone. Then, usually, someone must go down, assess the victim's injuries, treat those that prevent evacuation, and attach the hauling line. With four or five people on top, and the lip of the crevasse well padded, it is sometimes possible to haul someone bodily out of the crevasse. If that is impossible, a Z-pulley system must be rigged to provide the rescuers with a mechanical advantage. The first step is setting a bombproof anchor. Then use a prusik knot or ascender to tie off the fallen climber's rope to that anchor. This prusik knot holds the climber's weight while the pulley system is moved after reaching the limit of its travel. After passing through the prusik knot, the rope from the fallen climber is threaded through a pulley on the anchor, then led back along the climbing rope to the moving pulley, which is attached to an ascender fastened to the climbing rope, as shown in the diagram. The final leg of the Z leads to the people who will do the pulling. Inserting a belay plate between the "ratchet" prusik knot and the pulley will keep the prusik knot from jamming the pulley. If an ascender is used, a sling running from an ice ax to the ascender will serve the same purpose, as shown in the diagram. It's a good idea to practice setting up and using this system before you venture onto McKinley.

This setup provides a mechanical advantage of three to one. Three feet of rope must be hauled in to raise the fallen climber one foot, but a force of one pound exerted on the hauling end puts three pounds of force on the climber. For example, let's say a force of 300 pounds is required to overcome friction and lift a heavy climber out of a crevasse. Using a Z-pulley system, a team of climbers would have to exert a force of only 100 pounds on its end of the rope to generate the force needed to complete the rescue. The system also magnifies the force applied to the anchor, which must be able to hold hundreds of pounds. Rescuers must be careful not to pin the fallen climber against the overhanging lip of the crevasse. At the first sign of increasing resistance, someone on top must ensure that the victim can either push away from the overhanging lip, or has the strength and time to chop the lip down to a manageable size.

Teams of two need to think very carefully about crevasse rescue before venturing onto the most dangerous McKinley glaciers, such as the East and Northeast forks of the Kahiltna and the Peters Glacier. If one member takes a bad fall into a crevasse, the climber on the surface will probably find himself supporting the fallen climber's full weight from his harness while sprawled out in self-arrest position. From that position, the would-be rescuer must somehow fashion a solid anchor, attach the fallen climber's rope to the anchor with a prusik, then assist the fallen climber out of the crevasse. If the fallen climber is injured, the climber on top must haul his partner to the surface by himself – an extremely difficult proposition. Teams of two are always more vulnerable than larger groups in the event of an accident, but perhaps nowhere more so than while approaching the technical climbing on a heavily crevassed glacier. As a minimal safety precaution, a team of two should use a 165-foot rope. Before tying in, each climber should coil up about 60 feet of rope and loop it over his shoulder. That leaves the two climbers about 45 feet apart, with enough spare rope available for each to reach his partner should he go into a crevasse. Each climber should carry adequate anchoring hardware, three prusiks or ascenders (one for each foot, one for the pack), several slings, half-a-dozen carabiners and two pulleys clipped to his harness.

Sleds complicate glacier travel because they can skitter off snow bridges and into crevasses, and can land on top of a climber who has fallen into a hole. In two crevasse falls on McKinley, a sled that landed on top of a fallen climber contributed to the accidents' fatal outcome. It's a good idea to attach the tail end of the sled to the climbing rope with a prusik to prevent it from going in after the fallen climber. It's important to attach the sled to the rope at just the right point, particularly if you attach the sled hauling lines to your pack. If the attachment point of the sled to the climbing rope is too close to you, you'll wind up tugging on the rear end of the sled with the climbing rope. On the other hand, if you attach the sled too far away

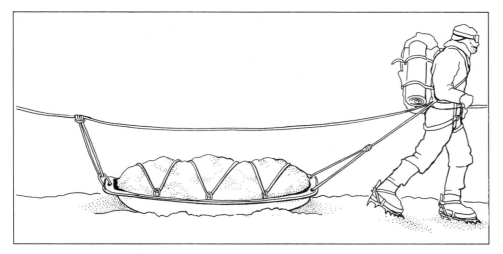

A climber hauling a sled is safest when both the climbing rope and sled traces are taut.

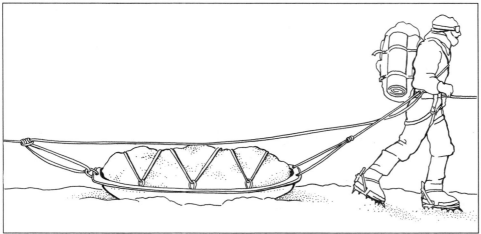

The excessive slack in the climbing rope means that, in the event of a cravasse fall, the climber would be hanging from the sled traces.

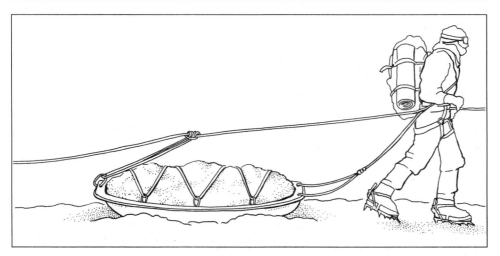

When the sled traces are slack, the climber is pulling on the rear of the sled with the climbing rope, which causes the sled to yaw from side to side.
Drawings: Marj Leggitt

from you, you could end up hanging from the sled, via your pack harness, rather than hanging from your climbing harness – a potentially dangerous situation. Be sure gear is securely lashed to the sled. Losing your tent, sleeping bag or stove off the sled and into a crevasse during a fall would probably end your trip.

Attaching the sled to the rope doesn't protect the last climber on the rope, who has two options in dangerous areas: dispense with the sled, perhaps by carrying a heavier pack (to equalize the work load among team members), or attach the sled to the rope in front while crossing dangerous bridges, allowing the climber in the lead to drag the sled through the stretch where the climber bringing up the rear is most vulnerable.

At all rest stops in which the climbers gather together, the rest area must be probed thoroughly, preferably with something longer than an ice ax. An inverted ski pole works well if the snow is soft; a pole with the basket removed works better, particularly if the snow is firm. Each climber after the first should be belayed as he arrives; the first climber on each rope should be belayed as he leaves.

Establishing a camp also begins with probing. The path to the camp latrine must also be probed. After probing, the perimeter of the camp should be wanded and the wands respected. One unfortunate climber took a single step outside the wanded perimeter of his camp on the Muldrow Glacier and fell 130 feet to his death in a hidden crevasse.

Stamping out tent platforms and building snow walls to protect the tents from wind comes next. Wait a few minutes after stamping out the tent platform and the snow will age-harden as the crystals re-bond to one another in their new configuration.

With luck, the surface snow will be firm enough to permit block-cutting. If it's not, dig down until it is. Sometimes stamping will consolidate the snow enough to permit block-cutting for snow walls and igloos near the surface.

Snow walls become increasingly important with each step upward in elevation. Winds almost anywhere on the mountain, but particularly at Windy Corner and above 15,000 feet on any route, can be strong enough to erode the corners and edges of snow blocks until the wall collapses. Pouring water over the blocks, for climbers with the fuel and patience, bonds the blocks together into an ice-hard mass. Don't underestimate the wind's ability to knock down a flimsy snow wall. Once, while trapped in a windstorm at 17,200 feet on the West Buttress, I built a wall with blocks so big I could barely lift them. Despite the strenuous effort, the wind toppled the wall repeatedly that night. The next morning I rebuilt my crumbling fortress, this time setting the rectangular blocks so their long axis was perpendicular to the previous configuration, creating a Maginot Line about two feet thick that was finally able to withstand the continuing gale. It took so much work to build I was tempted to auction it off when I left.

Always stake your tents securely! In 1983, a tent blew past some climbers camped at 8,000 feet on the West Buttress. A couple of hours later, a group of climbers showed up and asked which way the tent went. They had pitched it at 10,000 feet and failed to anchor it well. One ice ax doesn't constitute secure anchoring. The minimum should be three solid anchors; four is preferable. Skis, ski poles with the baskets removed, snowshoes, ice axes, pickets, dead men and stuff sacks filled with snow and buried are all good anchors.

Igloos, while time-consuming to build, provide great shelter in bad weather. They are quiet, sturdy and absorb condensation. However, depending on the elevation, location and season, they can collapse when the sun comes out again. Igloos are generally safe above 14,300 feet at any time of year.

Building igloos well requires practice. The basic principle is to lay down a sturdy, circular foundation of blocks, then carve it down to form a circular ramp whose high point butts up against the low point. Succeeding layers of blocks are built upward in a spiral rather than in concentric circles. By building in a spiral, each new block is supported on both the bottom and one side as it is laid in place. Usually, each block must be individually carved to shape. Fitting the final blocks into place requires a person on the inside. The floor of the entrance tunnel should be lower than the level of the sleeping area. This makes the igloo warmer and helps stop spindrift.

Digging snowcaves is a hard, wet, cold job, but the security they provide, particularly up high, often makes them worth the effort. The best site is usually a hillside facing away from the prevailing wind, although the vortices that form on the lee side of a ridge just below the crest can fill even a cave that faces directly away from the storm's onslaught. Beware of caving below cornices, both because of the avalanche danger, and because of the spindrift problem.

You can make the task of cooking outside more pleasant and efficient by building a sheltered kitchen area surrounded by a snow-block wall. Wherever you plan to cook, collect clean snow in a stuff sack, then set up the stoves and get them roaring. Long before the last chore is done, most climbers are eagerly anticipating dinner and drinks. Hot liquid is the nectar of the gods after the sun goes down, and thirsty climbers need a lot of it. That's one reason meals and camp chores in general take far longer than most people expect. Breaking or making camp, including a meal, easily takes three to four hours. Chores can take even longer up high, where the cold forces climbers to stop frequently to warm their hands, and where even simple tasks make climbers pant like broken-down mules. Climbers should take into account the time required for chores when they're estimating how much time they have to climb each day and how many days the route will require. It's common on McKinley for climbers to overestimate the technical difficulty of the terrain, but to underestimate how long the route will really take.

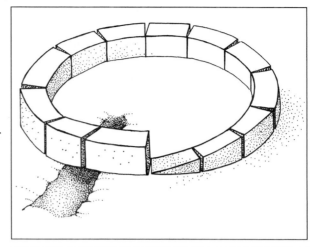

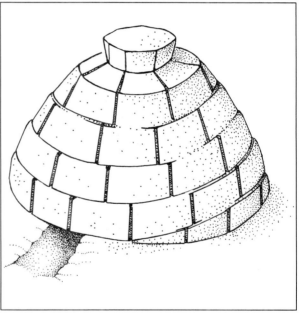

Top: After laying down the first row of snow blocks, use a snow saw to create the "ramp" shown here. The trench juttin out to the left can be the quarry for some of the blocks. When complete, the trench serves as the entranceway. Bottom: To complete the igloo, shape a capstone block to fit and set it gently in place.
Drawing: Marj Leggitt

Climbers ferrying loads on McKinley face one final and unexpected problem: ravens. These tough, intelligent and powerful birds can wreak havoc on a cache, consuming an amazing amount of food and scattering much of the rest. They go through sturdy nylon duffel bags like they were paper, and plastic bags like they weren't there. Caches have been attacked all the way up to 16,400 feet.

Mounding snow over a cache is a poor solution because the wind can erode away the snow, and because ravens apparently have learned that unusual snow mounds mean food. Ravens will dig into even the best-covered cache if they know it's there. The only solution up high is to find a nook in the rocks and cover the cache with stones. The best solution on the glacier is to dig a pit deep enough so that the food will be covered by at least one foot of snow when the pit is refilled to the glacier surface level. In June and July, when melting causes the surface of the glacier to drop rapidly, dig a pit deep enough to allow the food to be covered by two feet of snow when the hole is refilled. Don't leave a mound of snow as a target for the wind or an invitation to these voracious birds. Mark the cache with wands bearing a piece of tape with your expedition name, the date the cache was made and the date of your expected return. You don't want anyone to think the cache has been abandoned. Set the marking wands a measured 10 feet straight north of the cache (or in some other easily remembered direction). Ravens may even be smart enough to associate a group of wands with your delectable edibles. As too many climbers have learned at a high cost, it doesn't pay to underestimate the raven.

Many climbers cache a bag of trash next to their skis at 11,000 feet on the West Buttress, planning to pick it up on the way down. This is acceptable only if the trash is buried very deeply (three feet or more) and you make absolutely certain you do indeed retrieve your trash cache during your descent. Too many people casually bury a bag of trash, fully intending to retrieve it later, then find upon their return that the glacier surface has receded, the trash has been exposed and the garbage has been scattered far and wide by wind and ravens.

Environmental
Considerations

McKINLEY'S POPULARITY HAS CREATED a serious trash and sanitation problem. At both 16,400 feet and 17,200 feet on the West Buttress, trash, feces and yellow urine stains dot the snow. Conditions at the Crow's Nest, as the bowl at 17,200 feet is called, are particularly disgusting. The rocky rim of the Crow's Nest offers an absolutely stunning view of Mt. Foraker, Mt. Hunter and the plains to the north of the range, but you'd better watch your step while you're admiring it: innumerable piles of shit dot the entire area. In June, 1992, climbing rangers and volunteers spent an entire day digging up frozen turds at 17,200 feet and carting them to a nearby crevasse. They also loaded up a giant bag with 600 pounds of trash and abandoned food and fuel caches. The load was carried out by helicopter. Abandoned gear, garbage and excrement mar the beauty of the few sheltered campsites on the West Rib and Cassin. Not even the winter storms cover these insults to the mountain. The winds are so high that the snow simply blows away.

The only acceptable solution to the trash problem is to pack it out – all of it, without fail, without excuses. This is a Park Service regulation, as well as common sense. Park Service rangers on patrol have ticketed climbers for littering. If you can carry wrappers and bags containing food on the way up, you certainly can carry empty wrappers and bags back down. Careful repackaging of food before the trip reduces the amount of trash created tremendously. A little effort before the trip will make your load lighter on the mountain and should reduce the amount of trash produced to less than five pounds per person for a three-week trip. Keep the trash dry (and therefore light) by stowing it in a large plastic bag or stuff sack. Cache the trash accumulated on the early part of the trip at the same place that you cache your skis or snowshoes, then pick it up on the way down. You'll find it surprisingly easy to move the trash downhill on a sled. Don't leave extra food or fuel behind on the theory that other climbers will use it, or that "You're planning to come back next year." Abandoned food dumps almost always become garbage as ravens and the wind scatter food and packaging materials far and wide. As mentioned in the chapter on group equipment, fixed lines, if used, also must be removed. Climbers considering a route that they think will require fixed lines are strongly encouraged to pick an easier route they feel they can do without fixed lines.

In the early days, climbers disposed of human waste by digging a deep latrine in the snow, then filling it in when they left. This practice is no longer acceptable. The number of climbers who camp at the popular sites is simply too high. Latrines dug in early season tend to melt out as the season progresses, exposing the waste on the surface. All drinking water on McKinley comes from melting snow. If everyone dug latrines, the odds would be appallingly high that later parties would find their drinking water contaminated by feces. In 1989, a climber was evacuated on a sled from 9,800 feet on the West Buttress with severe gastroenteritis that required surgery. He had probably contracted it by drinking melted snow contaminated with feces at 14,300 feet or 17,200 feet on the West Buttress.

To avoid these problems, everyone must follow these simple recommendations. At Kahiltna Base and at 14,300 feet on the West Buttress, the Park Service provides latrines. Please use them for both feces and urine. It's your own drinking water that you may be contaminating if you do otherwise. Elsewhere on the mountain, the basic solution to the sanitation problem is to collect the feces into a large plastic garbage bag, then dispose of the bag into a deep crevasse. When down low, dig a pit 18 to 24 inches deep and line it with a garbage bag. Cover the hole with a large snow block when not in use to keep it from filling with snow. Wands can be used to stake out the corners of the bag. Another good solution, particularly for larger groups, is a lightweight toilet seat mounted on a folding stand. The plastic bag can be clamped between the seat and the legs. Well-equipped sporting-goods and camping-supply stores stock various models. This solution makes it almost impossible to miss the bag. Tipping the seat on its side with the bag's mouth pointing away from the wind prevents the bag from filling with snow when not in use. Food scraps also go into the latrine bag. A three-gallon bucket lined with a large plastic bag can serve the same purpose as the toilet seat. When you break camp, throw the latrine bag into the nearest deep crevasse. It may be necessary to haul the bag on a sled for some distance to find a suit-

Folding toilet seat.
Drawing: Nancy Young

able crevasse. Since the contents are usually solidly frozen, you're unlikely to contaminate your sled. Be careful not to get too close to the lip of the crevasse. If undercut, it may not bear your weight. On steep routes, throw the latrine bag off the ridge, away from the climbing route, preferably toward sections of glacier that never receive climbing traffic. Alternatively, defecate onto a large snow block, then shovel the snow block off the ridge. Climbers should designate one spot at each camp for depositing urine.

Sanitation up high is a bigger problem because unprotected plastic bags quickly shred and fill with spindrift in the strong arctic winds. Try digging a hole, lining it with a plastic bag, then throwing in a snow block to keep it from blowing away. Close the latrine bag after each use by twisting it shut, then weighting the neck of the bag with a snow block. For a deluxe alternative, use a storm or acclimatization day to build a latrine igloo or snow cave, then use the low-altitude procedure of digging a pit and lining it with a garbage bag. As always, toss the latrine bag into a deep crevasse or off the steep side of the ridge. At 17,200 feet on the West Buttress, walk downhill to the northeast, toward Denali Pass, and throw your latrine bags into the large crevasse there. The Park Service is considering various ways to improve the sanitation situation at 17,200 feet. Check with the rangers for the latest recommendations before starting your trip.

In really severe conditions, when using a plastic bag is impossible, defecate directly on the snow. When the weather moderates, shovel the now-frozen feces into a plastic bag and deposit it in a crevasse. Don't leave your waste sitting there to mar the enjoyment and threaten the health of the next group of climbers. Rangers have ticketed climbers for improper sanitation procedures. They are determined to continue enforcing sanitation and litter regulations vigorously.

Camp at 11,00 feet on the West Buttress.
Photo: Glenn Randall

*Cloud Cap over
McKinley's summit as
seen from camp at
17,200 feet.*
Photo: Glenn Randall

Climate

FROM THE JOURNAL OF MICHAEL COVINGTON, chief guide for Fantasy Ridge, June 5, 1980:

"Today we descended from our camp on the West Rib at 16,000 feet to 11,200 feet on the West Buttress in what was one of the most terrifying days I have ever spent in the mountains. By the time we arrived at camp below Windy Corner (12,500 feet), the gusts were in excess of one hundred miles per hour and gusting once every twenty seconds. The effort and likelihood of getting a wall up (to shelter a tent) was equivalent to the risk and effort of getting to a lower elevation, so we continued to descend. The winds continued to increase as we continued down. One of the gusts knocked all nine of us to the snow. I got up quickly during a brief lull and completely to my surprise I was swept into the air and flew until my rope came tight. That gust must have been in excess of 150 mph. I don't ever recall a feeling of such helplessness in the mountains. Had it not been for the fact that most of the rest of the team were still trying to get up, it's quite possible we all could have been swept off the mountain and down onto the Peters Glacier several thousand feet below."

On June 15, 1947, on the Harper Glacier, the temperature reached -20 degrees F and the wind blew 50 mph, producing an effective wind-chill temperature of -101 degrees F. During a cold snap in May 1982, temperatures at 17,200 on the West Buttress routinely reached -40 degrees F. Blessedly, the wind was calm. The strongest wind measured on McKinley came crashing past Windy Corner at 87 mph. That's not likely to have been the strongest gust that has occurred. Winds in excess of 100 miles per hour have been reported more than once.

In June 1981, six feet of snow fell in one day at 17,200 feet. The next day, 100-mph winds stripped the camp of every flake. A group at 14,300 feet on the West Buttress reported nine feet of snow in two days. Drifts reached 12 feet on the South Buttress in just a few hours, forcing the climbers to abandon their camp.

Conversely, on the lower Kahiltna, temperatures have reached 65 degrees F even in the shade. On July 4, 1968, the temperature in the sun on the Kahiltna reached a stupefying 136 degrees F.

These extremes define the limits of what climbers on McKinley can expect during the normal climbing months of April through July. Winter extremes are far worse. The temperature on the summit of McKinley at 7 p.m. on March 1, 1967, was -59 degrees F, with a 20 to 30 mph wind. That night, at Denali Pass, the wind increased to more than 100 miles per hour. Glacier pilot Don Sheldon reported that his airspeed gauge read 140 miles per hour while his plane held steady with a nearby ridge. The estimated temperature at 17,200 feet was -40 degrees F; the wind chill was -148 degrees F.

Much of the best data on McKinley's climate comes from an article in the 1971 *American Alpine Journal* (American Alpine Club Press). Information was based on records kept during six expeditions undertaken by different groups. The following information is based on that report.

Temperatures in direct sun average 30 degrees F higher than those in the shade. Sunshine also decreases the wind chill effect by 50 percent. The difference between a sunny day temperature taken in the shade and the nighttime temperature averages 15 degrees F on the Kahiltna, 11 degrees F on the upper West Buttress. Remember that the daytime reading was taken in the shade; the difference in the feeling on the skin from noonday sun to midnight shade may be the same as a drop of 45 degrees F. Cloudy periods exhibit less of a day-to-night contrast. The ice bowl at 14,300 feet on the West Buttress shows particularly extreme temperature swings because it acts as a reflector oven during the day and a cold-air sink at night. Low wind speeds at 14,300 feet increase the severity of the nighttime cold. The higher average wind speeds at 17,200 feet can bring up relatively warmer air from below, so that the lowest temperature recorded on McKinley is often at 14,300 feet.

Half of the observations on the West Buttress above 15,000 feet, and 60 percent of the observations on the Muldrow above that elevation, showed a wind-chill-equivalent temperature cold enough to freeze exposed flesh within one minute. As Bradford Washburn rightly observed, all movements above 15,000 feet on McKinley are totally dependent on weather.

Basically, three types of stormy weather occur on McKinley. As the season progresses, more and more cyclonic storms (low pressure systems) brew in the Aleutians and lash out across the Gulf of Alaska. Occasionally, the high pressure system commonly found over Hawaii moves north, shifting the Aleutian storm track from eastward to northeastward. In that situation, Aleutian storms descend upon McKinley with a vengeance. Weather records in Anchorage and Fairbanks show that precipitation in May is typically half that of June, only a third that of July. High cirrus clouds and rising wind precede the full fury of these cyclonic storms by about 12 hours. Precipitation is always heaviest on the southern side of the range. Talkeetna, for example, gets 30 to 35 inches of rain per year. Wonder Lake, north of the range, gets 10 to 12.

A second kind of bad weather is the low-level scud that tends to form during warm days, particularly later in the season. These clouds envelope the mountain up to, at most, 12,000 feet. Weather higher on the mountain may be superb. These low-lying clouds are formed by water evaporating off the lower glaciers and the rivers and lakes south of the range. As the prevailing wind brings that moist air in contact with McKinley's massive uplift, condensation begins and clouds form. Climbers down low sometimes find themselves toiling upwards hatless, with bare arms, as a feathery snow sifts down out of a hazy sky.

The third kind of stormy weather is among the most feared because it can strike so suddenly. Whenever the wind exceeds 20 miles per hour, a lenticular cloud cap can form over the summit. Often, the winds tearing through a lenticular cloud are far stronger. Lenticular clouds are named for their shape, which resembles the cross-section of a lens. The change from blue sky to whiteout can occur in 15 minutes. Lenticular clouds are present on McKinley more than 30 percent of the time. These clouds may look innocuous to an Alaskan novice, but the veteran knows that climbers are risking their lives to approach the summit when it is smothered by a lenticular.

Weather hinders climbers or confines them to their tents on about one day out of three on the Kahiltna. Up high, weather curtails activity for two days out of three. Only one day out of five, on average, is really clear. Washburn's 1949 expedition recorded only five days with more than 12 hours of clear skies in the three months it was on the mountain.

Weather spells, both good and bad, tend to come in cycles. In 1969, for example, the average length of each was four days. Storms up high can last 10 days or more. Storms of that length frequently have lulls, but when the storm returns, it can do so with little warning. One day out of three provides good flying weather. One out of the three is marginal; the third is hopeless.

No one month can be considered perfect for climbing on McKinley. April has a higher percentage of clear days, but the price is severe cold, higher average wind speeds and less daylight. On April 21, the sun rises at 3:56 a.m. and sets at 7:55 p.m. at park headquarters. The hours of genuine darkness discourage climbers from starting to move in mid-afternoon. The cold means that few avalanches or cornices fall due to the sun's warmth, but winter slab-avalanche conditions can present a hazard.

May is generally warmer than April (although still very cold), with a bit more precipitation and a bit less wind, on average, and more daylight. On May 21, the sun rises at 3:14 a.m. and sets at 10:33 p.m. The oblique path of the sun relative to the horizon means sunsets and dawns are lingering. By late May, only a few hours are truly dark. The sun can be hot enough to create instability in both steep snow slopes and cornices, but it also tends to consolidate those low-level slopes that don't avalanche by subjecting them to frequent freeze-thaw cycles. On some routes, it is possible to wait a few days after a storm for the sun and avalanches to work over a dangerous slope until it is stable, then cross it at night in complete safety. Technical routes in both April and May tend to have more ice, sometimes overlain with powder snow, and less névé, compared to later in the season.

June continues the trend toward warmer days, more frequent storms and greater daylight. Sunrise on June 21 is at 2:09 am; sunset is at 11:46 p.m., but no time is completely dark. Climbing is possible at any time, so climbers can take advantage of clear spells whenever they occur. Cornices totter towards spontaneous collapse. Climbers can no longer rely on the nights to be cold enough to re-freeze sun-loosened slopes and snow bridges at lower elevations. The greater warmth causes glaciers to move faster, which increases the frequency of ice falls from hanging glaciers and seracs.

By July, daylight once again begins to diminish, with sunrise at 3:18 a.m., sunset at 10:44 p.m. on July 21. Crevasses yawn wide and storms are frequent. Travel on the lower glaciers is sloppy and difficult, and rain may fall. The Kahiltna base camp is dismantled sometime during the month, as traffic on the mountain diminishes and the glacier surface becomes cupped and rutted, making landing difficult. Many of the cornices have fallen off, so that steep narrow ridges, now covered with névé, can actually be easier to negotiate than they were in May.

These guidelines are simply rules of thumb. McKinley can be beset with unbelievably bad weather and astonishingly good weather in any month of the season. Some climbers walk up their chosen route in constant sunshine and think the mountain a snap; others are hounded by constant storms and return proclaiming McKinley the coldest mountain on earth. Most get a taste of both, and return full of wonder at McKinley's beauty when the weather is good, and full of respect for its malevolence when the weather is bad.

Sunset on Mt. Foraker as seen from 14,300 feet on the West Buttress.
Photo: Glenn Randall

Getting to the Mountain

WHEN AT LAST THE PLANNING, training, food-packing and gear-testing are finally over, the journey to the mountain begins. The sense of unreality that can pervade preparations for a climb seen only in photographs is dispelled. For most climbers, an overwhelming excitement takes its place. Even for the most experienced – perhaps particularly for them – the excitement is mingled with a healthy dose of respect, even a tinge of well-controlled fear, for they know that McKinley in a savage mood is one of the most inhuman places on earth.

Two or three months before you actually pack your bags, write to Denali National Park and let them know you're coming. The address is in Appendix A. At present, there are no restrictions on the number of parties that can attempt McKinley at one time. To avoid confusion, use an expedition name and have one person handle all the correspondence with the Park Service and your pilot. In turn, the Park Service will ask each person to fill out a registration form. Registration is required only for climbs on McKinley and Foraker, although it is recommended for other climbs and ski tours in the park as well. When you get to Talkeetna, Park Service regulations require you to sign in with the Park Service and attend an orientation program that lasts about half an hour before flying in. Orientations are offered only during normal business hours. The rangers in Talkeetna are all experienced mountaineers who can offer much good advice. Most have done a number of routes in the range, as well as taken part in many rescues. More than one climber owes his life to their quick, efficient action. In addition, the rangers maintain a library of Washburn photos of the range, along with books and articles describing various routes. When you return from your climb, be sure to sign out.

Climbers can get to Alaska by flying to Anchorage, or by driving or taking a series of buses up the Alaska Highway to the Tok Cut-Off and Glenn Highway, which lead to Anchorage, or by taking the ferry from Seattle or Prince Rupert, British Columbia, to Haines, Alaska, then driving or taking a bus to Anchorage.

The Alaska Railroad and several shuttle services provide transportation from Anchorage to Talkeetna, the jumping-off point for the West Buttress and other routes on the south, west and east sides of the range. The Alaska Railroad also goes to Denali National Park headquarters, last stop for those planning to do the Muldrow or other routes on the north side. The Alaska Railroad runs only a limited number of times per week in early season, so be sure to ask about schedules in advance.

Talkeetna is a quaint but growing town of perhaps 300, with restaurants, motels, bars, a grocery store and a few arts-and-crafts shops. Prices are even higher than is normal in Alaska, and selection is very limited, so don't plan on buying expedition food in Talkeetna. Camping is free at various sites around town. At this time there is no bank in Talkeetna, so be sure to bring an adequate supply of cash or traveler's checks.

Dale Atkins, Larry Palubicki and Chris Melle get ready to fly into Kahiltna Base with pilot Jim Okonek.
Photo: Glenn Randall

Climbers have spent as little as a few hours and as long as two weeks in Talkeetna, waiting for the weather to permit their pilot to fly them to the glacier. Waits typically are only a few days in early season; they get progressively longer, on average, in June and July. To establish priority, make a reservation with a pilot well before arriving in Talkeetna and put down a deposit. The cost round-trip to Kahiltna Base in 1992 was about $230 per person. Four air taxi services operate out of Talkeetna. One operates out of the town of Denali Park for climbers planning to approach the mountain via the Muldrow or Peters glaciers or for those who wish to fly to Kantishna (a tiny hamlet just north of Wonder Lake) before the road to Wonder Lake opens. Wonder Lake is the starting point for the hike across the tundra to the Muldrow and Peters Glaciers. Addresses for air taxi services are in Appendix A.

Climbers who wish to attempt the West Buttress, the south face routes, (Cassin, West Rib, etc.) or the South Buttress from the east fork of the Kahiltna all fly from Talkeetna to Kahiltna Base, 7,200 feet, on the southeast fork of the Kahiltna Glacier. A radio operator paid by the pilots is stationed there during May and June. The operator monitors CB channel 19 24 hours a day. Climbers flying in very early or very late in the season should make special arrangements with their pilot about getting picked up again.

Climbers attempting routes on the southeast and east sides of McKinley usually fly in to the west fork of the Ruth Glacier. During good weather, pilots fly over the Ruth frequently as they transport climbers to and fro and conduct aerial sight-seeing flights for tourists. Most climbers carry a CB to communicate with them.

Flying is not the only way to get in to the southern and eastern sides of McKinley. A few teams have started at the end of the Petersville Road and walked up the Kahiltna, a distance of at least 40 miles. This road opens to four-wheel drive vehicles about the first of June. Climbers who wish to ski in before the road opens have to start from the Parks Highway, which adds more than 26 miles.

Other teams have started from the Parks Highway at about milepost 130 and skied or snowshoed up the Ruth Glacier, a distance of at least 30 miles. Most teams opting for an approach on foot hire a pilot to fly in a load of supplies to either Kahiltna Base or the west fork of the Ruth. Air support is only allowed outside the old (pre-1980) park boundaries. That boundary cut through the range between McKinley and Mt. Hunter, making Kahiltna Base and the west fork of the Ruth the closest practical, legal landing sites for McKinley. When the boundary was pushed further south, the Park Service continued to allow pilots to land at their traditional landing sites. This regulation, which is supported by both climbers and pilots, maintains the wilderness character of the mountain itself, yet also makes the south side of the mountain much more accessible than it would be if climbers had to approach from the road.

The south side of the range is quite brushy. The large and turbulent rivers can be a formidable obstacle after the ice breaks up. The best time for a land approach is in April, when frozen creeks provide unobstructed travel routes for those on skis or snowshoes. In July, 1978, I hiked out down the Tokositna Glacier after climbing Mt. Huntington. The trek took five grueling days, as we wound our way through crevasse fields, battled through alder thickets rife with spiny devil's club, and forded waist-deep swamps while beset by clouds of mosquitoes, all the while burdened with awesome packs. Purists who want to approach by land instead of air probably will find a hike over the tundra north of the park to be far more enjoyable.

On the north side of the range, the old park boundary was drawn far to the north of the base of the mountain. Climbers doing north-side routes must either walk in from Wonder Lake, a distance of 19 miles, or else fly in to Kahiltna Base, cross Kahiltna Pass at the head of the Kahiltna and descend the heavily crevassed Peters Glacier. No air drops are allowed anywhere within the park.

Climbers going in to the Muldrow or other north-side routes face a dilemma. Travel across the tundra is much easier in early April, when rivers are frozen and skis or snowshoes can be used while hauling a sled. Once on the mountain, however, April can assail the climber with bitterly cold and windy weather. North-side routes get little sun at that time of year. Temperatures moderate as the season progresses, but foot travel on the tundra becomes much more difficult, the mosquitoes swarm and all the weight must be packed on your back, making load-ferrying mandatory. Crossing the McKinley River can also become one of the most difficult sections of the trip.

One solution is to hire a dog musher to freight in supplies in early season and cache them at McGonagall Pass. Climbers can go in then or later. A cache left for any length of time must be bear-proof and odorless. The address of the only outfit licensed to haul in supplies, Denali Wilderness Enterprises, is in Appendix A.

The road to Wonder Lake usually opens in late May or early June, so climbers planning to go in earlier must either fly to Kantishna, just north of Wonder Lake, or ski in from the Parks Highway, a distance of 85 miles.

Glacier pilots most commonly use single-engine, four-passenger Cessna 185s or the equivalent. Remove anything lashed to the outside of your pack, like your sleeping pad or ice ax, so that the pilot can pack your gear more easily into the tight confines of the fuselage. The 40-minute flight to Kahiltna Base is spectacular, so photographers should keep their cameras handy. Don't open the window for a clearer shot, however, without asking your pilot first. After landing, move your gear well away from the plane. Often the pilot will need a push to get his plane turned around. Be sure to hang on to anything light, like a sleeping pad or coat, when the pilot revs up the engine. The prop blast during take-off is enough to blow lightweight gear quite a ways. When the spindrift settles again and the plane has become a speck against the mountain walls, the expedition will have truly begun.

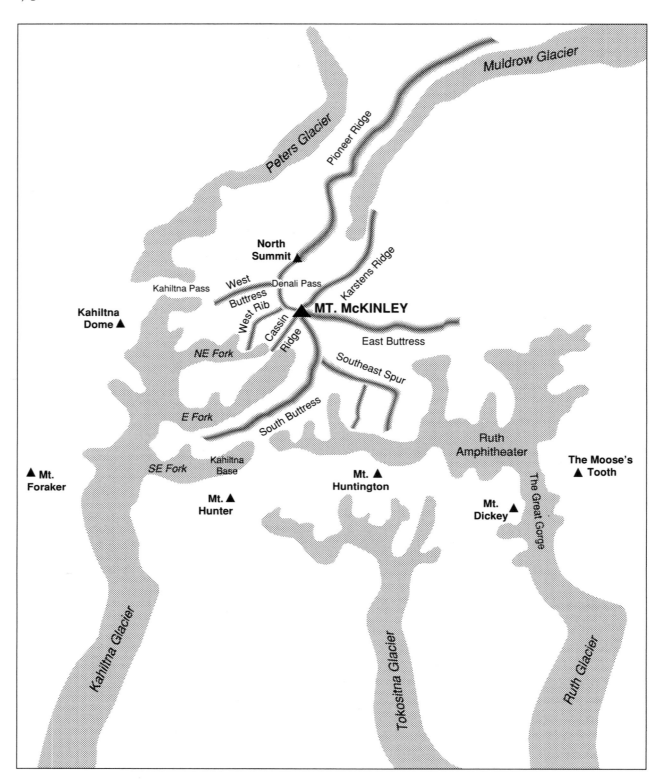

McKinley's routes and ridges.

The West Buttress

THE WEST BUTTRESS IS BY FAR the most popular route on McKinley. Roughly three-quarters of the 1,000 or so climbers who attempt the mountain each year choose that route. About 50 or 60 percent succeed. Some people are lured into a false sense of security because other climbers are often in sight. Some find the absence of total solitude annoying or disheartening. Others, though, – probably the majority – feel that talking to the other teams and learning about the far-flung corners of the world from which they come are half the fun of climbing McKinley. Those seeking solitude should climb one of the many rarely traveled ridges and spurs on the other sides of McKinley's complex bulk.

Some people call the West Buttress a walk-up. Usually, those people have never been on the route. The West Buttress deserves respect, not only because of McKinley's height, extreme cold and ferocious weather, but because several of its slopes are steep enough to kill people who fall off them. Already, there have been a number of serious falls resulting in injuries requiring evacuation on the "easy" 30-degree slope leading to Denali Pass. The slope from 15,000 to 16,000 feet is much steeper, although there are normally fixed lines there placed by guides.

The times given here are approximately correct for those moving uphill with a substantial load. Exceptionally strong climbers can undoubtedly move faster, although if they do so too many days in a row, they will gain altitude too quickly for their bodies to acclimatize. Climbers hindered by bad weather or the need to break trail after a storm or in early season – or those packing unusually heavy loads – might well take half again as long. The times given allow for brief rest stops but not extended siestas. The downhill times assume travel on foot or snowshoes. Competent skiers experienced in traveling roped together will need less time than the amount given here.

Elevations given refer to Bradford Washburn's map of Mt. McKinley, which no McKinley climber should be without. A black-and-white excerpt of this map appears on pages 90 and 91 of this book. The complete map is available in the United States for $12, plus $2 postage and handling, from University of Alaska Press, First Floor Gruening Building, Fairbanks, AK 99775-1580. It also is available in Europe from the Swiss Foundation for Alpine Research, Binzstrasse 23, 8046 Zurich, Switzerland.

Most climbers approach the West Buttress expedition-style, in which they make two trips up each section of the climb, carrying half their gear, food and fuel each time. A few tackle the route alpine-style, carrying everything with them in a single push. For climbers starting with 20 days of food, that means moving between 80 and 100 pounds of gear per person during the first few days. With a heavy sled and a heavy pack, it can be done, but few people find it worth the pain. A few people cut down both their safety margins and their chances of success by taking less food. For most people, seventeen days is about the minimum that allows sufficient time for acclimatization. The most likely result of taking much less is a severe case of mountain sickness. Few climbers start up the route with more than 25 days of supplies.

Nearly all West Buttress climbers fly from Talkeetna, at 300 feet, to Kahiltna Base, at 7,100 feet on the southeast fork of the Kahiltna. The southeast fork is used instead of the main Kahiltna because it gives the pilots a downhill airstrip for take-off. The large slit latrine at the west end of camp helps keep the camp clean. Please use it for both feces and urine, but not trash. Many climbers pass through Kahiltna Base every year. Everyone must pitch in to keep Kahiltna Base from degenerating into a pig sty.

From Kahiltna Base, the West Buttress route leads west, downhill, for one mile to the main Kahiltna. This 350-foot hill makes a great downhill ski run at the start of the trip, but tired climbers slogging back up it after the expedition have given it the name that stuck: Heartbreak Hill.

At the base of Heartbreak Hill, at 6,750 feet, turn north, up the main Kahiltna. Be careful not to cut too close to Mt. Frances, the peak in the northeast corner of the junction of the two glaciers. Large crevasses scar the glacier at Mt. Frances' foot. The mountain was named for Frances Randall, a concert violinist from Fairbanks who manned the Kahiltna Base radio for many years. She died of cancer in 1984.

Once on the main Kahiltna, continue north to the 7,000-foot contour, the base of the first steeper rise in the Kahiltna and site of a major set of crevasses. The safer but longer route is to pass these crevasses to the west. A route on the east side, cutting close to the northwest buttress of Mt. Francis, can also be found, particularly in early season.

After either route, regain the center of the glacier and continue north to the large level area at 7,700 feet below Ski Hill, which rises steeply, gaining about 1,000 feet in the next mile and a quarter. The level area at 7,700 feet, five miles from Kahiltna Base, is an excellent campsite. With full loads, most climbers take from four to five hours to reach this site from Kahiltna Base. The return to Kahiltna Base for another load (for those relaying loads, expedition-style), takes about two or three hours.

A long band of crevasses running north and south, parallel to the main flow of the Kahiltna, leads up the middle of Ski Hill. The normal route skirts these crevasses to the east. Ski Hill gradually loses its steepness and Kahiltna Pass (10,320 feet) slowly comes into view. There's no need to go to the pass itself. The glacier flattens out 400 feet below the pass, forming a good campsite. Winds through Kahiltna Pass can be strong; this is a good place to start building sturdy snow walls around the tents. The distance from the 7,700-foot camp to the Kahiltna Pass campsite is about 3¼ miles; the elevation gain, 2,300 feet. For a loaded-down team, this takes four to six hours.

Although only two campsites have been mentioned on the Kahiltna, in reality camps can be placed almost anywhere after thorough probing for crevasses. Camps in the middle of the steeper sections simply require more digging to make level tent platforms.

From just below Kahiltna Pass, turn east, up an unnamed fork of the Kahiltna, and climb to a small basin at 11,000 feet. Two or three hours are usually required for this 1,000 feet of elevation gain.

Give careful consideration to the threatening seracs looming on the slopes above before situating the camp at 11,000 feet. Debris below several of them shows them to be active.

Most people leave their skis, snowshoes and sleds behind at this camp. Steeper climbing and higher winds above this point normally make crampons and ice axes the most useful tools. In late season, however, with the heavier snowfalls, sleds and skis or snowshoes can be useful over parts of the route leading to the ice bowl at 14,300 feet. Sleds are usually more useful above 11,000 feet than skis or snowshoes. Only expert skiers should try to ski downhill through the crevasse field at Windy Corner while carrying a full pack and trailing a sled. I still remember panicking and screaming at my rope mate to stop as he built up speed to cross a crevasse. The insistent tug on the rope was forcing me to accelerate out of control down a steep drop with a 40-pound sled pursuing me like a NFL tackle. Trying to ski downhill around Windy Corner with a full load is asking for trouble.

Anything cached at 11,000 feet should be well-marked with double-length wands (two wands taped together). This camp is known for particularly heavy snow accumulations. Put your expedition name and the date on the wands marking the cache.

From 11,000 feet, the route trends northeast, up Motorcycle Hill (called Squirrel Hill by some), the headwall that climbs 500 feet to the crest of a ridge, which is sometimes called Lunch Rocks. This ridge can be considered the lowest part of the West Buttress itself. From the ridge crest, the route heads east, keeping north of the rocky ridge crest. Views to the north, down to the Peters Glacier and out to the tundra, are spectacular. Anything dropped off a sled or pack on this section will probably quit rolling 2,000 feet below.

At 12,200 feet, the ridge ends at the lower edge of a broad, windswept plateau. The rocky foot of the true West Buttress lies directly ahead. From here, head southeast toward Windy Corner, the shallow notch between the rocky foot of the West Buttress and the 13,350-foot hump just to its west. The lip of the crevasse at 12,900 feet, just below Windy Corner, is sometimes a good campsite, depending on how the crevasse has filled with snow. Another good campsite can, with work, be chopped out of the slope just below the crevasse. Both sites are somewhat sheltered from the worst of the Windy Corner gales and are safe from avalanches pouring off the 3,000-foot walls of the West Buttress, but neither would be a happy camp in a severe storm. Don't camp lower in the basin than the 12,900-foot bergschrund. Caches and camps at about 12,500 feet and 12,700 feet have been hit by avalanches. Most groups take two to four hours to reach the plateau from 11,000 feet and another two hours from the plateau to Windy Corner.

The next good campsite (after the one at 11,000 feet) is the ice bowl at 14,300 feet. For most people, however, 3,000 feet of elevation gain at that altitude is a long day. One solution is to carry the heaviest possible cache to Windy Corner one day, then try for 14,300 feet the next day with the bare essentials for a camp, returning on the third day to pick up the cache. Another solution begins with moving the cache as before. The next day, weather permitting, move the whole camp and dig in for one night at Windy Corner, then finish moving the camp to 14,300 feet the next day. On the fourth day, return to Windy Corner to pick up your cache. If at all possible, avoid camping for two nights in a row at Windy Corner. Betting that the weather will remain stable that long is gambling against long odds.

After turning Windy Corner, head east again, skirting along the foot of the West Buttress' southern flanks, staying above the shattered ice field just below. This area is one of the most heavily crevassed on the entire route. The steep gullies scoring the West Buttress can drop avalanches during or immediately after a heavy snowfall or during a hot afternoon. Rockfall is also a possibility.

Rob Dubin at 16,600 feet on the West Buttress.
Photo: Glenn Randall

Continue to hug the foot of the West Buttress, trending slightly to the north as you climb through the 14,000-foot contour. Pass the large crevasses just below the 14,300-foot camp to the north. Groups commonly take from eight to 12 hours to climb from 11,000 to 14,300 feet.

The ice bowl, despite its elevation and apparent defenselessness before southwesterly storms, actually is one of the most sheltered camps on the West Buttress. The summit cloud cap rarely reaches that low; the low-lying scud rarely reaches that high. That's not to say strong winds can't strike, but the generally moderate weather makes this site an ideal place to rest and acclimatize before moving into the much harsher world above 16,000 feet.

Most groups that succeed in remaining healthy take from five to nine days to reach 14,300 feet. Five is minimum; for some people, it is too little. They become sick and must descend. Anything less than five days creates a high probability of illness. Most groups find that spending several nights at 14,300 feet makes the big jump to 17,200 feet much easier.

From 14,300 feet, the route looms overhead, ominous yet exciting. Head north, toward the notch in the West Buttress at 16,000 feet. The first 1,000 feet of this slope can avalanche after a heavy snowfall. In July, 1951, during the first ascent, Bradford Washburn's team found waist-deep snow all the way to the bergschrund.

The steepest climbing on the West Buttress, a consistent 45 degrees, lies between 15,000 and 16,000 feet. Several sets of fixed ropes provide a measure of additional security, but none should be trusted completely, even after thorough testing. Wind, sun, crampon teeth and ice ax picks and spikes destroy fixed line with remarkable speed. In July, 1951, Washburn found this slope to be solid blue ice covered with a veneer of snow. In those days, before front-pointing, chopping each step required 20 to 30 blows.

The best procedure for using the fixed line is to run a sling from an ascender clipped to the line to a carabiner on your harness. Use one hand to slide the ascender upward; use the other on your ice ax. Don't use the fixed line to pull yourself upward or to rappel on the descent. It's simply not that trustworthy.

A majestic vista of tundra and glacier greets climbers as they crest the ridge at 16,000 feet and look north. The black rocks of the North Peak come into view for the first time. The route goes east, up the ridge crest, staying generally to the northern side. This rocky ridge provides the most airy, exposed climbing on the route, though nowhere can it be considered technically difficult by modern alpine standards. A campsite can be chopped out at 16,000 feet at the top of the fixed lines. A natural site exists at about 16,400 feet. Both lie naked before McKinley's winds, and would be a bad place to get caught by a storm. Two tents have literally blown off the ridge with their occupants tumbling about inside like frightened dolls in a clothes dryer gone mad. Fortunately, no one's been killed, though two climbers were evacuated by helicopter after one incident. The shallow, wind-hardened snow would make snow caving difficult. Ravens have attacked caches even this high, so bury caches well with rocks or snow.

The West Buttress proper ends at the Crow's Nest, the saucer-shaped plateau at 17,200 feet. Most climbers camp along the saucer's western rim where the slight slope makes cave digging easier and the rocks on the saucer's lip create a slight wind-break. Building a snow cave or igloo to back up even a heavily fortified tent site is well worth the energy, both for safety and peace of mind. Climbers reaching the Crow's Nest soon after other climbers have descended should look for abandoned caves and igloos.

The eight- to 12-hour day from the ice bowl at 14,300 feet to the Crow's Nest taxes almost everyone. Most teams break the move into two days by carrying a load of food and fuel to 16,000 feet or higher, then descending to spend another night at 14,300 feet. On the day they move camp, they take only three or four days of food, just enough to make it to 17,200 feet that day, reach the summit (they hope) the next and descend the third. If weather or the need for acclimatization prohibits a summit bid with that limited amount of food, climbers drop back down to their cache to replenish their supplies. The weather a few hundred feet below the Crow's Nest is often markedly better than the weather 1,000 feet above. Strong climbers just take their cache all the way to 17,200 feet on the first day, then move camp up the second. It's common for climbers to wait three to five days or longer at 17,200 feet before the weather finally relents and allows them to try for the summit.

Some climbers take three days to move themselves and their supplies to 17,200 feet. They carry a load to 16,000 feet or more on one day, then return to 14,300 feet for the night. The next day, they dig a campsite at the lip of the bergschrund at about 15,000 feet. On the third day, they move camp to 17,200 feet. This strategy reduces the elevation gain on the day climbers move camp to 17,200 feet by one-fourth, a significant difference at that altitude. Camping at 15,000 feet for one night also aids acclimatization slightly more than does another night at 14,300 feet, reducing the shock to the body of a 3,000-foot altitude gain. The campsite at 15,000 feet is scarcely more exposed to wind than the one at 14,300 feet. Space is somewhat limited and a fair amount of work is required to chop out tent platforms. A warning: This site has been hit by avalanches during storms. In addition, huge hidden crevasses lurk in the area. Camp at 15,000 feet only with great caution.

From the Crow's Nest, the route follows a gradual rising traverse to 18,200-foot Denali Pass, visible directly to the east. Even in late June, this north-facing slope is shaded in the early morning. Toes and fingers commonly suffer from the cold. Although pitched at an angle of only 30 degrees, the snow can be so wind-hardened that a slip not checked immediately can turn into a cartwheeling fall.

The wind rules at Denali Pass. Sometimes, but not always, it diminishes as climbers turn south and head up the broad, ill-defined ridge above. Be sure to wand the route well from here to the summit, if it is not already wanded. The route generally stays to the east of the actual ridge crest. It passes west of the Archdeacon's Tower and descends slightly to a broad plateau, facetiously called the Football Field, at 19,600 feet. The true summit is in view at last, only 700 feet above. The headwall from 19,600 to 20,000 feet is best tackled on its west side, where the angle is slightly less. Once the summit ridge is gained at 20,000 feet, turn east and climb the final 300 feet to the small, well-defined, 20,320-foot summit.

Reaching the summit from 17,200 feet takes from six to 10 hours. Descending takes between two and four hours. The descent is by far the most dangerous portion of the summit day, particularly the descent from Denali Pass. Carrying an ice ax to the summit and back is essential, so climbers can self-arrest if they slip. Don't make the mistake of taking only ski poles. Splitting up the team on the summit day often has been the prelude to an accident. The strength of a united party might have saved several of the lives that have been lost above Denali Pass. Don't bivouac above 18,000 feet. Too often that has led to frostbite, hypothermia and death. If you don't think you can make the summit that day, turn back and try again another day. You may find that the extra time spent acclimatizing at 17,200 feet will allow you to reach the summit in a reasonable amount of time a few days later.

Most teams take a day to descend from 17,200 feet to 14,300 feet, then finish the descent the next day. Others, though, driven by thoughts of hot showers, fresh fruit, salads, nachos and beer, descend all the way to Kahiltna Base in one long day.

Beyond The West Buttress

THE WEST BUTTRESS, DESPITE ITS POPULARITY, is by no means the only good, technically moderate route on McKinley. The Muldrow, although much longer, requires a similar level of technical expertise. Neither route requires the ability to climb steep, hard ice or difficult rock. Other routes of great beauty but low technical difficulty are the South Buttress, which starts from either the west fork of the Ruth or the east fork of the Kahiltna, and the upper portion of Pioneer Ridge above the Flatiron Spur. Pioneer Ridge borders the Muldrow Glacier. Both of these routes are long and isolated. Climbers should expect to spend longer up high than is required on most other routes. Injury, illness or equipment breakdown on McKinley's isolated routes is an even more serious problem than on the West Buttress.

McKinley's other ridges and faces abound with long, technical routes demanding a full range of mountaineering skills. Not only must climbers be sure and swift on steep ice and rock, they must be able to negotiate the difficulties while carrying a hefty pack. The Southeast Spur and East Buttress, and their variants, such as Reality Ridge, offer a number of difficult ways to try for McKinley's summit on a side of the mountain that sees very little traffic. The Northwest Buttress, which leads only to the North Peak, is perhaps the safest of the difficult routes. Both routes on the Wickersham Wall are threatened by avalanche danger and are not recommended.

The magnificent Cassin Ridge, which divides McKinley's south and southwest faces and leads directly to the summit, is considered by many experienced alpinists to be the route to do on McKinley. The West Rib is easier than the Cassin because its difficulties are less sustained and there is little or no rock to deal with, depending on the exact route chosen. However, the West Rib remains a challenging route, demanding extensive experience on ice, at high altitude and in the cold. Other routes on the south face, such as the American Direct, Scott/Haston, Milan Krissak Memorial and Czech Direct, must be ranked with the Southwest Face, the Isis Face and the Ridge of No Return as among the most difficult routes McKinley has to offer. The Isis Face and the Ridge of No Return are on the south side of the South Buttress.

Two of the best published sources for information on McKinley routes are the *American Alpine Journal* and the *Canadian Alpine Journal*. Volumes of the *AAJ* dated 1971 to the present have an index of routes described in that volume. A master index is available in some libraries for previous years. *The Mountain World*, published from 1953 to 1969, also has articles covering some McKinley climbs. The American Alpine Club library in Denver has reference copies available. Other libraries that have mountaineering collections may also have these volumes.

Peter Metcalf works his way up Reality Ridge.
Photo: Glenn Randall

Climbing, Summit and *Mountain* magazines are not indexed, but the staff may be willing to dig out back issues containing information on McKinley routes. The Park Service can provide up-to-date information on what has and hasn't been climbed. Sometimes, it can also provide the names and addresses of the climbers who did the first ascent.

Perhaps the best source of information is close study of the extremely sharp aerial photographs taken by Bradford Washburn. Like any distant photos, they can make a route appear easier or more difficult than it actually is. Obstacles that appear minuscule in the photos may actually be overhanging ice cliffs 75 feet high, as Peter Metcalf and I discovered during the first ascent of Mt. Foraker's Highway of Diamonds. Profile shots of ridges, for example, don't reveal how sharp the ridge is and to what extent it is corniced. Head-on shots obscure the true steepness. Try to compare photos from as many different angles as possible. Bear in mind that the scale of the Alaska Range is vastly greater than anything in the Lower 48. Only after several climbs in the range can climbers get a really accurate sense of what a route will be like by looking at even the best photos. Many of Washburn's photographs, overlaid with lines indicating the routes, have been published in Jon Waterman's *High Alaska* (American Alpine Club Press, 1988). The book also contains basic route information, such as elevation gain, the elevation of potential camps, estimated total time and a brief description of the technical difficulties.

The most popular routes on McKinley, after the West Buttress, are, in order of increasing difficulty, the Muldrow, South Buttress, West Rib and Cassin. Taken together, these five routes account for over 98 percent of the traffic on McKinley. The campsite elevations given in the route descriptions that follow are approximate.

Muldrow Glacier
Wonder Lake is the starting point for climbers intent on doing the Muldrow. Climbers starting the route in early season either fly to Kantishna and ski or snowshoe the six miles to the south end of Wonder Lake, or ski in a distance of 85 miles from the park entrance to Wonder Lake, using dog teams for support. In summer, after the road to Wonder Lake opens, climbers take the park shuttle bus to the south end of the lake. Private cars are generally not allowed on the Wonder Lake Road. Except in early season, temperatures are warm enough on the tundra that food like cheese can spoil before climbers reach the colder weather of the glacier. The tundra is grizzly bear country, so food caches left temporarily while load-ferrying must be completely odorless. Backpackers and climbers in the northern area of the park generally are required to carry food in bear-proof containers issued by the park. However, that requirement is waived for climbers approaching the Muldrow.

Still, elementary precautions should be followed. Don't cook in your tent. Cooking odors can permeate the nylon and draw bears even if you stash your food elsewhere. Don't cook and camp in the same spot. Instead, cook a meal, then move on a mile or two before camping. Don't store food in your tent. If possible, hang it in a tree. Make noise when you walk, so you won't startle a bear that's unaware of your presence. Denali National Park rangers can provide literature with more detailed recommendations.

The major obstacle on the 19-mile hike from Wonder Lake to McGonagall Pass, the start of the glacier travel, is the McKinley River. Expeditions have been so intimidated by this turbulent torrent that they have turned around at its banks, which lie only two miles from the highway. Water levels are lowest in early season. Water levels also fluctuate during the day, usually peaking in mid-afternoon.

In 1980, Bradford Washburn surveyed the best route from Wonder Lake to McGonagall Pass and published the results on a special map, which, unfortunately, is no longer in print. The following description is based on that map. You'll need USGS maps McKinley A1, A2, B1 and B2, all published in 1954 at a scale of 1:63,360, or about an inch to the mile. Your route won't actually touch all four maps, but they'll help you identify landmarks. The Washburn map of McKinley doesn't extend north of McGonagall Pass.

It would be helpful to have your topo maps in front of you to fully understand the description that follows.

Start from the road about a half-mile east of the Wonder Lake campground and head almost due south to the McKinley Bar, a broad, braided stretch of the McKinley River. Pick your way across following a southeast bearing, then head south and southwest to Turtle Hill, a 2,804-foot bump that's 6.2 miles from Wonder Lake. Pass Turtle Hill just to the east and continue south, working your way past dozens of ponds and lakes, until you intersect and cross Clearwater Creek just west of a pronounced northward bend in the creek. This crossing point is about one mile east of the junction of Clearwater Creek and Cache Creek and about 10 miles from Wonder Lake. Travel west along the south side of Clearwater Creek for a half mile, then turn south again, skirting the west side of the Lower Moraine. Intersect and cross Cache Creek where the Lower Moraine makes a sharp jog to the east. Continue almost due south, gradually moving closer to Cache Creek, which parallels your course to the east. Cross Cache Creek at mile 13.4, then continue south along the creek, crossing it several more times, to McGonagall Pass, 19 miles from Wonder Lake. Be prepared for mosquitoes and heavy brush. Wildlife abounds on the trek to McGonagall Pass, so boil or treat all water, even runoff from snow banks.

The easiest way up the lower part of the heavily crevassed and changeable Muldrow Glacier is usually along its right side. After five miles, climbers must negotiate the Lower Icefall. Usually the right (west) side is least shattered, although that route is mildly threatened by a hanging glacier on the flanks of Pioneer Ridge. Above the Lower Icefall, the route picks its way to the base of the Great Icefall, which is skirted on the right (west). The route avoids the Harper Icefall by climbing to Karstens

Notch, at the base of Karstens Ridge, and following the ridge and the Coxcomb above to the Harper Glacier at 15,000 feet. Karstens Ridge and the Coxcomb are the crux of the route, with slopes reaching 35 to 40 degrees that can be icy in early season. One good campsite exists on the ridge at 12,100 feet.

The route winds through the icefalls on the Harper Glacier to Denali Pass and follows the West Buttress route from there to the summit. The Muldrow route commonly takes 21 to 35 days, round-trip. Most climbers descend by retracing their steps and returning to Wonder Lake. A few descend the West Buttress and fly out from Kahiltna Base. Powerful winds funnel through Denali Pass and rake the Harper Glacier, so well-built tent walls, snow caves or igloos are a necessity. Don't camp right at Denali Pass. The wind is likely to make mincemeat out of your tent.

South Buttress

Start the South Buttress from either the west fork of the Ruth Glacier or Kahiltna Base. The Ruth Glacier start gains the crest of the buttress from the extreme west end of the west fork of the Ruth Glacier, then follows the crest of the buttress to the base of the southeast face at 15,570 feet. A few narrow sections, one 1,000-foot 45-degree snow and ice slope, and a large cornice blocking the ridge, are the major problems encountered on this section of the climb. The first-ascent party negotiated the cornice by locating a natural tunnel leading through it.

From Thayer Col, at 15,570 feet, a variety of routes are possible on the southeast face, all of which go up snowfields linked by moderate snow-covered rock bands and couloirs. These slopes lead to the summit ridge in the vicinity of the peaklet marked 18,960 feet. The summit ridge is mostly a walk, although it narrows and steepens somewhat just below Carter Horn. From Carter Horn to the summit is another 100 feet of elevation gain.

A second way to approach the South Buttress gains the crest from the east fork of the Kahiltna via a 4,000-foot, avalanche-prone ramp. Both slab and serac avalanches occasionally rake this moderately dangerous slope. The ramp joins the South Buttress route previously described at 15,600 feet. Climbers going alpine-style on either variant usually leave the glacier with ten or 12 days of food. Expedition-style attempts can easily take 15 to 25 days from either landing site. Climbers either descend the route or the West Buttress.

West Rib

Climbers approach the West Rib via the northeast fork of the Kahiltna, known as the Valley of Death because avalanches sweeping down from the Windy Corner hanging glacier and the Kahiltna Peaks can cover the entire glacier. Four climbers vanished in the Valley of Death in 1980. Only two marginally safe campsites exist on the northeast fork. One is at about 10,000 feet, on the top of a small hill just before the icefall at the base of the West Rib. The other is at about 12,200 feet on the far east side of the valley, which avoids the runout path of a hanging glacier on McKinley's southwest face.

Difficult climbing on the West Rib begins in a 45- to 50-degree ice couloir just right (east) of the rib's initial rock. Several climbers have been hit by avalanches in this 1,500-foot couloir during the 24 hours immediately following a storm. The snow had accumulated in the shallow basin at the top of the couloir. A bivouac can be made on a ledge at the top of this couloir, but there is no room for a tent.

Above the couloir, the route follows the rib's crest up less steep snow and ice to 13,300 feet, where the ridge broadens and flattens into a good campsite. Progress is easy until the rib steepens again at 14,000 feet, where there is also a good camp. Pitches of rock, ice and snow alternate to 18,000 feet, where a broad snow couloir starts and leads to the summit plateau and the West Buttress route at 19,400 feet. Climbers then follow the West Buttress route to the summit. Decent camps are at about 14,800 and 16,400 feet. Teams climbing alpine-style usually leave the glacier with eight to 12 days of food. A traverse can be made from the West Buttress at 14,300 feet to the West Rib at 16,000 feet. Some teams start up the West Buttress and climb only the upper half of the West Rib.

Descent, for those who wish to carry their camp up to the junction with the West Buttress at 19,400 feet, is down that route. Other teams descend the West Rib to 16,000 feet after reaching the summit, then traverse to the West Buttress and finish their descent via that route.

Cassin Ridge

The Cassin Ridge may be approached from either the northeast fork or the east fork of the Kahiltna. The northeast fork approach leads directly to the base of the Japanese Couloir, considered by most climbers to be the crux of the route. The east fork approach is longer, safer, and requires climbing to Kahiltna Notch via an ice couloir, then rappelling 300 feet and traversing to the base of the Japanese Couloir at 12,400 feet.

The Japanese Couloir has sections of steep ice, mixed ice and rock and pure rock. It ends at a narrow ledge barely wide enough for a tent at 13,400 feet. Many parallel strands of fixed rope mar the Japanese Couloir. None should be trusted. A Japanese climber rappelling using an old fixed line in the couloir was killed in 1974 when the rope broke.

From the top of the couloir, three mixed pitches lead to a narrow ridge crest, which in turn leads to the hanging glacier at 14,000 feet and the best camp on the route. At 15,000 feet, mixed climbing begins again in the first rock band. A camp can be chopped out at 15,700 feet. From there, the route leads up and left to a 300-foot chimney/gully. A camp can be chopped out at 16,000 feet, at the top of the chimney. The route avoids the difficult rock immediately above by traversing to the right (south), then climbing a long, easy snow gully that regains the ridge crest at about 17,700 feet. A camp can be chopped out here. A bit better site is at 18,000 feet. The climbing above 18,000 feet goes over easy snow and snow-covered rock to the summit ridge. Depending on the exact line, climbers reach the summit ridge at 19,800 to 20,100 feet.

The Cassin Ridge is the most demanding of the frequently attempted routes on McKinley. A snow cave can be dug only at 14,000 feet, so carrying a sturdy tent is important. It's possible to traverse from the Cassin to the West Rib at approximately 16,500 feet, but this 40-pitch traverse on 40-degree snow and ice should not be taken lightly. During the first part of the traverse, would-be escapees need to find their way through or around rock bands. The rest of the traverse is potential slab-avalanche country. Two climbers fell off the traverse and were killed in 1990. Alpine-style ascents of the Cassin Ridge usually take eight to 12 days from the base of the Japanese Couloir. Descent is almost always down the West Buttress.

Rob Dubin and Larry Palubicki on the summit of McKinley.
Photo: Glenn Randall

Washburn Photographs

Everyone who embarks on an expedition to Mt. McKinley owes a debt of gratitude to Bradford Washburn, mountaineer, cartographer and aerial photographer extraordinaire.

Washburn's lifelong fascination with McKinley led him to create the first large-format collection of aerial photographs of the mountain. All of the photographs that follow were drawn from his files, which he started building in 1936. His photographs, combined with the ground-based data collected on three scientific expeditions, allowed Washburn and his team of cartographers to compile the extraordinarily accurate and detailed topographic map of the peak that no McKinley climber should be without.

Washburn's photos and enthusiastic articles describing new route possibilities inspired an entire generation of mountaineers to launch expeditions to the many ridges, spurs and buttresses that encircle McKinley's massive, complex bulk. During his expeditions, he climbed the peak three times, twice via the Muldrow and once via the first ascent of the West Buttress, a route he had discovered from the air. On his third ascent in 1946 (the first time the peak had been climbed three times by anyone), he was accompanied by his wife Barbara, who thereby became the first woman to climb McKinley. Other Washburn first ascents in Alaska are legendary. In 1937, glacier pilot Bob Reeve flew Washburn and Bob Bates in to Mt. Lucania, an unclimbed 17,150-foot peak in what is now Kluane National Park. Reeve's plans to bring in two more team members were foiled when slushy summer snow mired his plane on the glacier for five days. Reeve was finally able to take off, barely, leaving Washburn and Bates on their own. Throwing away every possible item of nonessential gear, including one of their two sleeping bags, they ran up Mt. Lucania and achieved the first ascent, then climbed 16,644-foot Mt. Steele, making the second ascent of that peak. Then, they drove themselves on a forced march on starvation rations to a trading post at Kluane Lake, 100 miles distant from their glacier landing site.

In 1991, at age 81, Washburn offered his explanation for why he and his wife had devoted half their lives to probing the secrets of the Alaska Range. "The answer is simple. There are few mountains of any size, anywhere on earth, that share McKinley's pristine beauty or offer the fascination of its rugged and exquisite wilderness approaches, its lush lowlands and rushing, icy rivers, its flora and its as-yet-unspoiled wildlife. Whether you first glimpse it at dawn from the gateway of the Chulitna Canyon or at twilight across Wonder Lake, you are caught spellbound by its grandeur and its aloofness from everything else that surrounds us in the hectic confines of our lower world."

The map of McKinley that appears on the following two pages is excerpted from the larger map surveyed by Bradford Washburn and produced by the Swiss Foundation for Alpine Research. Those interested in ordering the complete map should consult the appendix for further information.

An overview of the west side of McKinley shows the West Buttress, West Rib, Cassin Ridge and South Buttress. A close examination of the West Buttress route just above the 11,000-foot camp reveals an old foot trail. The current route follows the solid line.
Photo: Bradford Washburn, accession # 7267

NORTH PEAK

DENALI PASS

SUMMIT

CASSIN RIDGE

CROW'S NEST

14.300-foot CAMP

WINDY CORNER

WEST BUTTRESS

WEST RIB

11,000-foot CAMP

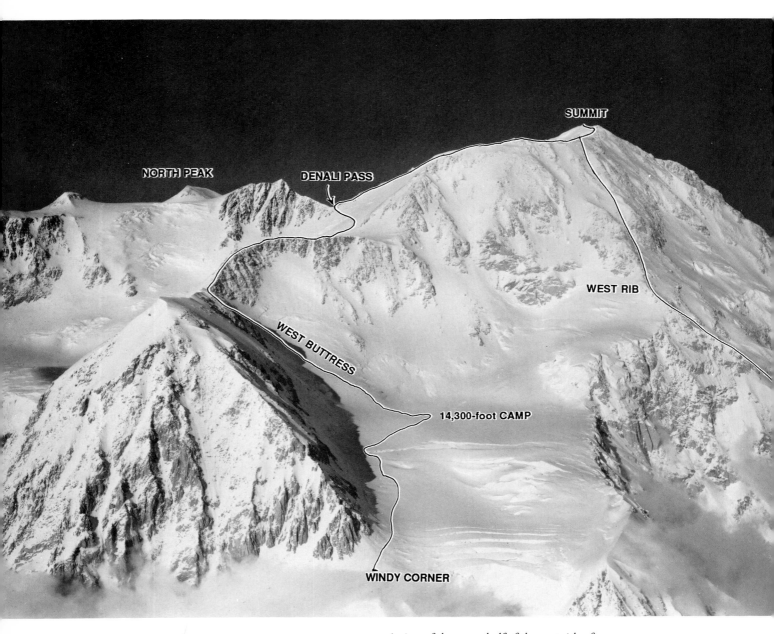

A view of the upper half of the west side of McKinley.
Photo: Bradford Washburn, accession # 5962

An overview of the Muldrow Glacier route.
Photo: Bradford Washburn, accession # 5220

The southeast side of McKinley.
Photo: Bradford Washburn, accession # 7013

*A view of the upper portion of McKinley
from the east.*
Photo: Bradford Washburn, accession # 5158

SOUTH BUTTRESS

The South Buttress Route. The variation shown starts from the west fork of the Ruth Glacier.
Photo: Bradford Washburn, accession # 5039

SOUTH BUTTRESS

*The South Buttress Route. The variation
shown starts from the east fork of the
Kahiltna Glacier.*
Photo: Bradford Washburn, accession # 8409

*A view of the upper half of the South
Buttress and the Cassin Ridge.*
Photo: Bradford Washburn, accession # 7200

14,300-foot CAMP,
WEST BUTTRESS

WEST RIB

A view of the lower half of the West Rib.
Photo: Bradford Washburn, accession # 4922

SUMMIT

WEST RIB

CASSIN RIDGE

The upper half of the West Rib and Cassin Ridge.
Photo: Bradford Washburn, accession # 4781

A view of the Cassin Ridge and the South Buttress.
Photo: Bradford Washburn, accession #5053

*The full moon rises over
Mt. Hunter at sunset.
Taken from 14,200 feet
on the West Buttress.*
Photo: Glenn Randall

Expedition Photography

Too many climbers start their expedition on McKinley intent on photographing every facet of the trip, then grow frustrated with that millstone of a camera hanging from their neck. They store the camera in their pack, pull it out to shoot a victory photo on the summit and find the camera frozen and useless. When they get home, they find they've shot only half a roll.

"Why didn't I shoot more pictures?" they lament when they see the processed film and realize that they have only a meager record of a rich and varied experience.

Following the three basic rules of high-altitude, cold-weather photography will prevent such disappointments. The rules are simple: Keep the camera accessible, keep it warm and keep it dry. Once you put your camera in your pack, you'll almost never take it out again while you're on the trail. The burden of shedding that massive pack, then putting it on again, quickly outweighs the value of a photograph in most people's minds. Putting the camera in the pack also lets it freeze. Keeping a camera dry, warm and available without driving yourself into hypoxic fits of frustration is the trick.

The easiest kind of camera to keep warm and handy is one of the many small point-and-shoot rangefinders available from all major camera manufacturers. These cameras are small enough to ride comfortably inside your coat without getting in your way. Beware of putting them in an inside pocket near your skin, then sweating hard. Moist air can penetrate the camera. When taken out in the cold, the moisture condenses inside the camera and lens, then freezes, potentially jamming the works. Cameras also can become damp through exposure to cooking steam or by snow melting on them. Store your camera in a small stuff sack or plastic bag if you're putting it deep inside your clothing. Use the same storage sack when you put the camera inside your sleeping bag at night.

Some point-and-shoots come with a fixed-focal-length lens, which can be rather limiting. More sophisticated point-and-shoots have zoom lenses of various types, which provide much greater versatility. Essentially all point-and-shoots are totally dependent on their batteries for all camera functions including metering and the shutter release. All types of batteries lose power in the cold. Keep your camera warm to conserve battery power, and carry several sets of spares. Look for models that give you some control over the exposure, such as an auto-exposure lock button.

As explained in more detail later, automatic meters are frequently fooled into underexposure on the brilliant white slopes of Denali. Point-and-shoots suit the needs of many less-serious photographers very well.

More fanatical shutterbugs probably will want to carry an SLR (single lens reflex) camera with an extra lens or two. Few SLRs can be relied upon to function perfectly in McKinley's severe cold if the camera is allowed to become chilled to the ambient temperature. For example, Olympus says that -4 degrees F is the lower temperature limit for reliable operation of its OM-1 and OM-4 SLRs. Professional models from some manufacturers may go lower, some as low as -40 degrees F. For most cameras, however, nighttime temperatures on McKinley routinely dip below the lower limits of reliable operation. Temperatures up high – even at noon – may cause problems. At temperatures lower than the camera's limit, lubricants thicken, springs weaken, and shutter and mirror movements slow as metal parts contract and bind. Note that these limits refer to the mechanical operation of the camera. Batteries begin to weaken long before the camera fails mechanically. The meter in an SLR is almost always driven by the battery. In more and more cameras, the shutter also uses battery power, as do a host of other camera functions, like autofocus. A camera with a battery-driven electronic shutter is useless if the battery has died, even if it's still functioning mechanically. As a general rule, nicad batteries work better in the cold than alkaline batteries. With some cameras, of course, you don't have a choice of what type of battery you can use. Always carry several spare sets in an inside pocket to keep them warm.

The camera will work best if it's kept warm and dry consistently. That means putting the camera inside your sleeping bag every night and keeping it under your coat on cold days. Even removing the camera from your sleeping bag and letting it lie around in the tent during breakfast may chill it so much that it jams at the first shot. As with a point-and-shoot camera, store your SLR in a plastic bag or waterproof stuff sack while it's in your sleeping bag or under your jacket. In extremely cold weather, cameras can freeze even under a shell. During an alpine-style ascent of McKinley's Reality Ridge in May 1982, I lost every photograph I took from 15,000 feet to the summit because the cold slowed the shutter and the camera overexposed every frame. I had slept with the camera and kept it beneath my wind shell, but to no avail with nighttime temperatures hitting -30 and -40 degrees F. I should have kept the camera under both my wind shell and the pile jacket that lay just beneath. Fortunately, the camera thawed on the summit day. The first properly exposed photos showed a weary but triumphant Peter Metcalf, ice ax pointed skyward, standing on the summit.

During the day down low, where temperatures are warm enough that I don't worry much about the camera freezing, I carry my SLR in a padded chest pack. Various commercial chest pack styles that come with their own chest harnesses are available. With these, you must remove the chest harness every time you change clothing, a procedure that becomes more tedious and annoying with each thousand feet of altitude gain. To avoid this frustration, I took an old zippered, padded camera case from LowePro (the exact model is no longer made, but similar items are available) and modified it to hang from my pack harness via one-inch side-release buckles. One strap runs from the righthand shoulder strap of the pack to the top right corner of the camera pack; another strap runs from the lefthand shoulder strap to the top left corner of the camera pack. A third strap runs from the pack waistbelt to the bottom of the camera pack to prevent bouncing while skiing. In effect, the chest pack serves as a substitute for a sternum strap. To take off the pack, I need only release the top left buckle, leaving the camera pack dangling from the right shoulder strap and waistbelt. I further modified the pack waistbelt so I could attach a couple of extra lens cases with another strap and side-release buckle. Cold does not affect extra lenses like it does a camera, although it does make the glue that holds the lens elements in place more brittle. Be especially careful not to drop a cold lens. The number of extra lenses I bring depends on the difficulty of the route and the importance of getting the best possible shot in every situation. A selection from medium-wide to short telephoto (or a zoom covering that range) will suffice for all but professionals.

Mt. Hunter from 7,700 feet on Kahiltna Glacier.
Photo: Glenn Randall

Up higher, when I need to keep the camera warm constantly, I stash it in the fold of fabric that forms just above my harness when I put my harness on over my wind shell. A loose-fitting shell with a full front zip makes this pocket large enough to accommodate even a full-size 35 mm camera. The camera is out of the way for climbing on slopes less than 55 or 60 degrees. I usually slip the camera into an unpadded stuff sack with a drawstring and cordlock to keep blowing snow that may enter the front of my jacket from melting onto the camera.

Other ways of carrying a camera have many drawbacks. Climbers on technical routes have so many gear slings and runners around their necks that trying to carry a camera slung over one shoulder using the camera's neck strap can create the threat of suffocation. The camera also quickly freezes and can be damaged easily.

Many companies now make small padded camera cases that ride on their own two-inch webbing waistbelt. These work fine in warm weather, but on McKinley, a camera carried in this fashion will freeze, even though the camera is close to your body. Another problem is the belt. Climbers on McKinley already have a pack waist belt and harness, plus, sometimes, a sled-hauling harness. These multiple layers of strapping pinch and chafe and jab as it is. Adding yet another belt to your already-crowded midriff can turn annoyance into misery.

When you do pull your camera out of its warm hiding spot for that once-in-a-life-time shot, beware of frostbiting your fingers. Up high, touching metal with your bare hands can freeze flesh almost instantly. Instead, learn to manipulate your camera with light gloves on.

I've never carried a tripod because of weight limitations, but I've also wished I had one for low-light alpenglow shots. Recently, I built a reasonably adequate substitute that uses adjustable ski poles with the grips removed as the tripod legs. Rather than carry a third ski pole, I use one of my partner's. The tripod head is a block of wood with three holes drilled in the bottom to accommodate the shafts of the ski poles. I drilled the holes at an angle, so the ski poles spread out just like a tripod's legs do. To attach the camera, I bolted a small ball head to the top of the block. The setup (minus the ski poles, which I carry anyway) weighs only 10 ounces.

The inside of a tent, with the sun shining on it, is plenty bright enough to shoot pictures without a flash if you can live with the pictures having a cast the same color as your tent fabric. Snowcave and igloo interiors are another story. If you want lots of pictures of that aspect of the trip, consider a flash.

Like a lot of professionals, I was a die-hard Kodachrome fan for many years. Lately, however, again like many pros who specialize in outdoor photography, I've switched to Fujichrome Velvia for its extraordinarily bright and vivid colors. Film becomes brittle in severe cold, so it's a good idea to keep the day's supply warm in an inside pocket. Be careful loading film, advancing it and rewinding it to avoid tearing the film sprockets or the film itself. Film that is already exposed or that won't be used immediately can be stored safely in your pack. Freezing will do it no harm.

Camera meters are all calibrated to give a correct exposure for more-or-less average subjects like skin, grass, trees and sky. Collectively, on average, these subjects reflect about 18 percent of the light that falls upon them. Unfortunately for the photographer, McKinley's brilliant white snows are far from average. They typically reflect anywhere from 75 to 90 percent of the light that falls on them. That means that if you trust your in-camera meter to give you the right exposure when the scene contains large amounts of snow, you'll seriously underexpose nearly all your shots. The most accurate, simple solution, in my opinion, is to let your camera meter off something that reflects 18 percent of the light falling on it. That something is called an 18 percent gray card, and it's sold in most good photo shops. A gray card is just that: a piece of stiff cardboard painted a medium gray. Before shooting a picture, hold the card so that the sun's light is falling directly on it, then meter off the gray card. Be sure your camera doesn't shadow the card. Lock that exposure into the camera's electronics by pressing the exposure-lock button or by putting the camera in manual mode and setting the exposure manually. Recompose and shoot. As an alternative to a gray card, you may be able to use your gloves or overmitts. Compare a reading taken from the gloves you'll wear while shooting to a gray card reading. Even if the two readings differ a little, you now know how to compensate when you're shooting. For example, if a gray card reading consistently shows an exposure a half-stop over the reading you get from your gloves, you'll know you need to open up half a stop whenever you use your gloves as a gray card.

This method works very well for front-lit and side-lit pictures. If you're shooting a portrait or a climber in action, avoid backlighting unless you're aiming for a silhouette. The best portraits almost always have most if not all of the person's face in the sun, or are shot in the shade against a shadowed background. In full sun, brimmed hats usually cause everything in the brim's shadow to vanish into black obscurity. When in doubt about the proper exposure, bracket by shooting at the meter reading, then two-thirds of a stop under and two-thirds of a stop over. If your camera is purely automatic, try fooling the meter by adjusting the film ISO setting when you want to bracket. For example, by setting the ISO at 32 when the film is actually rated 50, you'll be overexposing by about two-thirds of an f-stop. Bracketing ensures that you'll almost always get a pleasing exposure. I usually carry 15 rolls of film for a three-week McKinley expedition.

The ultraviolet or skylight filter that most photographers keep on their lenses at all times will work fine on McKinley. High altitude does not create a need for any special corrective filters. The sky is already so intensely blue that I have rarely felt the need for a polarizing filter.

The rewards of photography on McKinley easily outweigh the hassles of incubating your camera with all the care of a mother hen hatching an egg. Few non-climbers have any conception of what it's really like up there. Photographs reveal your experience to friends and family in ways that words never will. They also preserve your own memories for the rest of your life.

Camp at 7,700 feet on
the Kahiltna Glacier.
Photo: Glenn Randall

Appendices

Appendix A – Addresses

To request information on climbing McKinley, contact:

Denali National Park and Preserve
Talkeetna Ranger Station
P.O. Box 588
Talkeetna AK 99676
Ph. 907 733-2231
FAX 907 733-1465

The ranger station is staffed full-time from April through September, and intermittently the rest of the year. The South District Ranger lives in Talkeetna year-round.

The following companies offer transportation to Talkeetna from Anchorage. The 1992 cost for the shuttle services was about $40 per person one-way with a four-person minimum. The shuttle services will take smaller groups, but the charge per person is higher. In 1992, the Alaska Railroad charged $34.50 per person one-way, $69 per person round-trip after mid-May; early season fares were $25.50 one-way, $51 round-trip. Note that before mid-May, the Alaska Railroad offered only one train per week from Anchorage to Talkeetna. After mid-May, trains ran daily. Write or call in advance to determine the schedule during the time you plan to visit. Reservations are required.

Talkeetna Express – Mahay's
Box 705
Talkeetna AK 99676
Ph. 907 733-2223
FAX 907 733-2712

Denali Overland Transportation
Box 330
Talkeetna AK 99676
907 733-2384

The Alaska Railroad
Marketing & Sales Department
P.O. Box 107500
Anchorage AK 99510
Ph. 907 265-2494
From outside Alaska: 800 544-0552
FAX 907 265-2509

AIR TAXI OPERATORS:

These companies fly climbers from Talkeetna to routes on the south, east and west sides of McKinley:

Doug Geeting Aviation
Box 42
Talkeetna AK 99676
Ph. 907 733-3366
FAX 907 733-1000

Hudson Air Service
Box 648
Talkeetna AK 99676
Ph. 907 733-2321
FAX 907 733-2218

K-2 Aviation
Box 545
Talkeetna AK 99676
Ph. 907 733-2291
FAX 907 733-1221

Talkeetna Air Taxi
Box 73
Talkeetna AK 99676
Ph. 907 733-2218
FAX 907 733-2218

Denali Wilderness Air flies climbers from Denali National Park (the town) to Kantishna before the road to Wonder Lake opens in the spring.

Denali Wilderness Air
P.O. Box 82
Denali National Park AK 99755
Ph. 907 683-2261
FAX 907 683-1347

Some climbers planning to do the Muldrow Glacier or other north-side routes charter Denali Wilderness Enterprises to haul their supplies to McGonagall Pass or the foot of the Peters Glacier by dog-sled in March.

Denali Wilderness Enterprises
P.O. Box 30
Denali National Park AK 99755
Ph. 907 683-2644

These guide services are licensed to operate on Mt. McKinley and Mt. Foraker. Other guide services may have permits to lead trips in the new park additions.

Alaska-Denali Guiding, Inc.
Box 566
Talkeetna AK 99676
Ph. 907 733-2649
FAX 907 733-1362

American Alpine Institute
1515 12th St.
Bellingham WA 98225
Ph. 206 671-1505
FAX 206 734-8890

Fantasy Ridge Alpinism
Box 1679
Telluride CO 81435
Ph. 303 728-3546
FAX 303 728-3546

Rainier Mountaineering
535 Dock St., Suite 209
Tacoma WA 98402
Ph. 206 627-6242
FAX 206 627-1280

Mountain Trip
Box 91161
Anchorage AK 99509
Ph. 907 345-6499

National Outdoor Leadership School
288 Main St.
Lander WY 82520
Ph. 307 332-6973
FAX 307 332-3631

The Washburn map of McKinley is available in the United States for $12, plus $2 postage and handling, from University of Alaska Press, First Floor Gruening Building, University of Alaska Fairbanks, Fairbanks, AK 99775-1580 (Ph. 907 474-6389). It also is available in Europe from the Swiss Foundation for Alpine Research, Binzstrasse 23, 8046 Zurich, Switzerland. The map also is sold in many mountaineering stores.

You can order Bradford Washburn's magnificent black-and-white photographs of McKinley from:

Bradford Washburn
Museum of Science
Boston MA 02114-1099
Ph. 617 589-0228

As of July 1992, about three-quarters of Washburn's negatives had been transferred to the University of Alaska in Fairbanks. Washburn plans to transfer the remaining negatives during the next two to three years. Once the transfer is complete, orders should be placed with:

University of Alaska Fairbanks
201 Rasmuson Library
Fairbanks AK 99775-1005

Be sure to specify the negative number listed in the caption for each photo ordered.

Equipment supply shops in Anchorage:

Alaska Mountaineering & Hiking
2633 Spenard Road
Anchorage AK 99501
Ph. 907 272-1811

Gary King Sporting Goods
202 E. Northern Lights Blvd.
Anchorage AK 99503
Ph. 907 272-5401

Recreational Equipment Incorporated
1200 W. Northern Lights Blvd.
Anchorage AK 99503
907 272-4565

Appendix B – Personal Equipment

CLOTHING AND FOOTWEAR:

T-shirt (optional)
Nylon shorts (optional)
Two synthetic long underwear tops (one lightweight, one heavyweight)
Two synthetic long underwear bottoms (one lightweight, one heavyweight)
Vapor-barrier shirt (optional)
Pile pants or bibs
Heavyweight underwear top
Pile sweater or equivalent
Pile jacket
Wind parka and pants
Synthetic or down-filled parka with hood
Lightweight liner socks (two pairs)
Vapor-barrier socks (one pair)
Heavy wool or wool-blend socks (two pairs)
Camp booties (optional)
Lightweight liner gloves (two pairs)
Heavy gloves (one or two pairs)
Heavy wool mittens (one pair)
Nylon overmitts (two pairs)
Wool or pile balaclava
Neoprene face mask or lightweight balaclava
Dark sunglasses with side shields
Ski goggles
Nose guard for sunglasses
Knitted or pile ski hat or pile-lined, nylon shelled hat
Sun hat with skirt to protect neck (optional – most useful in June and July)
Bandana (optional)
Plastic double boots or vapor-barrier boots
Supergaiters or overboots if wearing double boots
Gaiters (for down low only – optional)

Sleeping:

Synthetic or down sleeping bag rated to -30 degrees F.

Vapor-barrier liner (optional if carrying a synthetic bag)

Two foam pads or one Therm-a-Rest and one foam pad

Gore-Tex sleeping bag cover (for down bags that don't have a built-in Gore-Tex shell)

Glacier Travel:

Skis with alpine-touring bindings to fit double boots or skis with three-pin bindings and very warm double touring boots (climbing boots must be carried also) or snowshoes

Climbing skins (for either kind of skis)

Waxes (for touring skis)

Ski poles

Sled or drag bag (most routes)

Technical:

Ice ax

Ice hammer (for routes with ice-climbing)

Seat harness

Chest harness

Crampons

Two ascenders or prusiks with foot slings, plus a third prusik to tie off a pack after a crevasse fall

Six carabiners, three slings (for crevasse rescue)

Two snow anchors for crevasse rescue (dead men or pickets)

Hammer holster(s)

Helmet (for technical routes only)

Other Personal Items:

Expedition-sized pack

Two wide-mouth one-liter bottles

Two insulated water bottle covers

Spoon

Cup

Bowl (optional)

Pocket knife (Swiss Army knife is handy)

Three butane lighters

Personal medical kit (aspirin, antacids, moleskin, etc.)

Toilet kit (toothbrush, floss, etc.)

Strong sunscreen (two four-ounce bottles per person)

Lip sunblock (three tubes per person)

Foot powder (optional)

Hand lotion (optional)

Lip balm (Chapstick, Carmex, etc.)

Books

Diary and pen or pencil (optional)

Camera, film and accessories (optional)

Extra stuff sacks

Strong elastic cords or straps with steel hooks (bungee cords or the equivalent) for lashing gear to sleds

Accessory straps (for lashing gear to packs)

Headlamp with extra batteries and bulbs (early season only)

Watch

Envelopes, stamps, writing paper, address list (optional)

Air-temperature thermometer (optional)

GROUP GEAR AND SUPPLIES:

Tent(s)

Stove(s)

Fuel

Cooking pot(s)

Pot grips

Scouring pad (optional – depends on menu)

Rope(s)

Wands

Rock hardware (for technical routes – nuts, pitons, carabiners, runners)

Ice screws (for technical routes – a couple are recommended for all routes in early season)

Map

Compass

Pocket altimeter (optional)

Radio (optional but recommended)

Spare batteries for radio (essential if bringing a radio)

Repair kit (see text for details)

Medical kit (see text for details)

Toilet paper (two rolls per person for the West Buttress)

Twelve large, heavy-duty plastic latrine bags

Food

Lighters

Matches

Snow shovel(s)

Snow saw(s)

Appendix C – Recommended Reading

The Ascent of Denali, Hudson Stuck, Scribner's, 1914, republished by The Mountaineers, 1977. Stuck's account of the first ascent.

Mount McKinley: The Pioneer Climbs, Terris Moore, University of Alaska Press, 1967. Excellent history of climbing on McKinley.

Minus 148: The Winter Ascent of Mt. McKinley, Art Davidson, Norton, 1969, republished in an expanded edition by Cloudcap Press, 1986. The gripping account of the first winter ascent.

Medicine for Mountaineering, fourth edition, edited by James Wilkerson, M.D., The Mountaineers, 1992. Excellent, comprehensive treatment of the subject. Consider bringing a copy on the expedition.

Mountain Sickness: Prevention, Recognition and Treatment, Peter H. Hackett, M.D., American Alpine Club, 1980. An in-depth discussion for laymen that should be considered required reading before attempting McKinley. Consider including a copy in the expedition medical kit.

Surviving Denali, second edition, by Jonathan Waterman, American Alpine Club Press, 1991. A sobering, well-researched study of accidents on McKinley from 1903 to 1990, written by a former Denali National Park ranger who is also a very experienced alpinist. The book is a must for McKinley aspirants.

High Alaska, Jonathan Waterman, American Alpine Club Press, 1988. An historical guide to McKinley, Foraker and Hunter, featuring a dazzling display of Bradford Washburn's aerial photographs of all sides of the three highest peaks in the range. Those seeking information on the less well-traveled sides of McKinley would do well to start with this book.

Glacier Travel and Crevasse Rescue, Andy Selters, The Mountaineers, 1990. Thorough, easily understood treatment of the intricacies of glacier travel and crevasse rescues.

Cold Comfort, Glenn Randall, Lyons & Burford, 1987. A detailed treatise on the art of staying warm in cold weather.

About The Author

GLENN RANDALL EMBARKED ON HIS FIRST EXPEDITION to the Alaska Range in 1978 at the age of 21. With three friends, he made the first ascent of Mt. Huntington's southeast spur, then walked out the Tokositna Glacier to the Petersville Road. Two years later, he returned with Peter Metcalf and Pete Athens and made the first alpine-style ascent of Mt. Hunter's south face (also known as the southeast spur). Two years later, Metcalf and Randall made the first alpine-style ascent of Reality Ridge, the western leg of McKinley's southeast spur, then climbed the southeast ridge of Mt. Foraker, the second-highest peak in the range at 17,400 feet. Later that same season, Randall guided a successful expedition on McKinley's West Buttress. Randall and Metcalf came back in 1983 to make the first ascent of Highway of Diamonds, a route on the north face of Mt. Foraker. In 1984, Randall guided unsuccessful attempts on the southeast ridge of Foraker and the West Buttress. During his most recent pair of expeditions, in 1987, he climbed Mt. Sanford, in the Wrangell-St. Elias Range, then joined an expedition attempting a ski descent of McKinley's Orient Express. During the expedition, he summited McKinley for the third time via the West Buttress.